A BORDERLESS BATTLE: DEFENDING AGAINST CYBER THREATS

HEARING

BEFORE THE

COMMITTEE ON HOMELAND SECURITY
HOUSE OF REPRESENTATIVES

ONE HUNDRED FIFTEENTH CONGRESS

FIRST SESSION

MARCH 22, 2017

Serial No. 115–9

Printed for the use of the Committee on Homeland Security

Available via the World Wide Web: http://www.gpo.gov/fdsys/

U.S. GOVERNMENT PUBLISHING OFFICE

26–907 PDF

WASHINGTON : 2017

CONTENTS

Page

A BORDERLESS BATTLE: DEFENDING AGAINST CYBER THREATS

Wednesday, March 22, 2017

U.S. HOUSE OF REPRESENTATIVES,
COMMITTEE ON HOMELAND SECURITY,
Washington, DC.

The committee met, pursuant to notice, at 10:18 a.m., in Room HVC–210, Capitol Visitor Center, Hon. Michael T. McCaul (Chairman of the committee) presiding.

Present: Representatives McCaul, Rogers, Perry, Katko, Hurd, McSally, Ratcliffe, Donovan, Higgins, Rutherford, Fitzpatrick, Thompson, Jackson Lee, Langevin, Richmond, Vela, Watson Coleman, Rice, Correa, Demings, and Barragan.

Chairman MCCAUL. The Committee on Homeland Security will come to order.

The purpose of this hearing is to receive testimony from cybersecurity experts on the evolving cyber threat landscape and the Department of Homeland Security's civilian cyber defense mission.

I recognize myself for an opening statement.

Today I look forward to discussing the borderless battle being waged against us by nation-states, hacktivists, and faceless criminals in cyber space. Last month I spoke at the RSA Conference in San Francisco, and my message today is the same as it was then: We are in the fight of our virtual lives, and we are not winning.

Our adversaries are turning digital breakthroughs into digital bombs. From Russia and Chinese hacking to brand-name breaches, our cyber rivals are overtaking our defenses.

Nation-states are using cyber tools to steal our country's secrets and intellectual property. Hackers snatch our financial data and lock down access to our health care records and other sensitive information. Terrorists are abusing encryption and social media to crowd-source the murder of innocent people.

Our exposure to cyber threats grows we understand the importance of not only being aware of each individual attack and piece of malware, but also the patterns of the sophisticated campaigns and life cycle of each threat.

It is clear that cyber attacks are becoming incredibly personal, and the phones in our pockets are now the battle space. Our most private information is at stake.

Just last week the Department of Justice indicted two Russian spies for their involvement in the hack of at least 500 million e-mail accounts at Yahoo. In 2015 Chinese hackers stole 20 million security clearances—including my own and many, I am sure, here in this room—in a breach of the U.S. Government's Office of Personnel Management. Recently an alleged attack of the CIA has WikiLeaks publishing over 8,000 pages of documents with some of the most highly sensitive cyber weapons.

Cyber criminals are targeting our wallets, as well. One of our witnesses today, General Keith Alexander, said on-line theft has resulted in the greatest transfer of wealth in human history.

Last year we also realized our democracy itself was at risk as the Russian government sought to undermine democratic institutions and influence our elections. They broke into political institutions, invaded the privacy of private citizens, spread false propaganda, and created discord in the lead-up to a historic vote.

The conclusion from all this chaos is clear: Our digital defenses need to be strengthened and our attackers must feel the consequences of their actions.

Unfortunately, the U.S. Government is fighting 21st Century threats with a 20th Century mindset and a 19th Century bureaucracy. Bigger Federal agencies are not necessarily the answer. We need to better tap into private-sector innovation, and more quickly.

But Government does play a critical coordinating role. When it comes to domestic cybersecurity it is important that our efforts are led by a civilian department, not by the military and not by intelligence agencies.

Just as we do not allow soldiers to police our city streets, we should not have organizations like the military or intelligence agencies patrolling domestic networks.

That is why in both 2014 and 2015 Congress passed legislation that I championed that better defined interagency cyber responsibilities. Those bills put DHS in the lead for operationally securing the so-called dot.gov space, helping to better protect critical infrastructure, being the hub for cyber threat information sharing, and providing voluntary assistance to private sector.

At the end of last year the Department announced it was providing cybersecurity services to 93 of the Executive branch's civilian work force. But perimeter detection is only one tool in our toolbox. We need defense-in-depth strategies and a talented cyber work force on the front lines.

Unfortunately, we are not attracting top cyber talent because morale is poor on the inside and money is better on the outside.

I propose the creation of a stronger, consolidated cybersecurity agency at the Department of Homeland Security. This will help us step up our cyber defense efforts and attract top talent, and we have already begun to work with the new administration and others to make that a reality in the near future.

Finally, winning battles in cyber space depends on our ability to deliver consequences. As a former Federal prosecutor, I know that if you don't make the costs outweigh the benefits, bad behavior will continue. This requires strong leadership and a willingness to track down rogue hackers, and a determination to hold hostile countries accountable.

Russia is the most immediate challenge. We cannot allow the Kremlin to get away with meddling in our democracy. We need a tough response, both seen and unseen, including tighter sanctions.

It is not just about what happened in 2016; it is about 2017, 2018, and beyond. Our adversaries are trying to break up the Western Alliance and interfere in other upcoming elections.

We have great witnesses here today to discuss all these threats, and I look forward to your testimony and recommendations.

[The prepared statement of Chairman McCaul follows:]

STATEMENT OF CHAIRMAN MICHAEL T. MCCAUL

MARCH 22, 2017

Today, I look forward to discussing the borderless battle being waged against us by nation-states, hacktivists, and faceless criminals in cyber space.

Last month I spoke at the RSA Conference in San Francisco. And my message today is the same as it was then: We are in the fight of our virtual lives, and we . . . are . . . NOT . . . winning.

Our adversaries are turning digital breakthroughs into digital bombs.

From Russian and Chinese hackings to brand-name breaches, our cyber rivals are overtaking our defenses. Nation-states are using cyber tools to steal our country's secrets and intellectual property.

Hackers snatch our financial data and lock down access to our health care records and other sensitive information. And terrorists are abusing encryption and social media to crowd-source the murder of innocent people.

As our exposure to cyber threats grows, we understand the importance of not only being aware of each individual attack and piece of malware but also the patterns of the sophisticated campaigns and the life cycle of each threat.

It is clear that cyber attacks are becoming incredibly personal, and the phones in our pockets are now the battle space.

Our most private information is at stake. Just last week, the Department of Justice indicted two Russian spies for their involvement in the hack of at least 500 million email accounts at Yahoo.

In 2015, Chinese hackers stole 20 million security clearances—including my own—in a breach of the U.S. Government's Office of Personnel Management.

And recently, an alleged hack of the CIA has Wikileaks publishing over 8,000 pages of documents with some of the most highly sensitive cyber weapons.

Cyber criminals are targeting our wallets too. One of our witnesses today, General Keith Alexander, said on-line theft has resulted in the "greatest transfer of wealth in history."

Last year, we also realized our democracy itself was at risk, as the Russian government sought to undermine democratic institutions and influence our elections.

They broke into political institutions, invaded the privacy of private citizens, spread false propaganda, and created discord in the lead-up to a historic vote.

The conclusion from all of this chaos is clear: Our digital defenses need to be strengthened—and our attackers must feel the consequences of their actions. Unfortunately, the U.S. Government is fighting 21st Century threats with a 20th Century mindset and a 19th Century bureaucracy.

Bigger Federal agencies are not necessarily the answer. We need to better tap into private-sector innovation—and more quickly. But Government does play a critical coordinating role.

When it comes to domestic cybersecurity, it is important that our efforts are led by a civilian department. Not by the military. And not by intelligence agencies.

Just as we do not allow soldiers to police our city streets, we should not have organizations like the military or intelligence agencies patrolling domestic networks. That is why in both 2014 and 2015 Congress passed legislation I championed that better defined interagency cyber responsibilities.

Those bills put DHS in the lead for operationally securing the so-called "dot gov" domain, helping to better protect critical infrastructure, being the hub for cyber threat information sharing, and providing voluntary assistance to the private sector.

At the end of last year, the Department announced it was providing cybersecurity services to 93 percent of the Executive branch's civilian workforce.

But perimeter detection is only one tool in our tool box. We need defense-in-depth strategies and a talented cyber workforce on the front lines.

Unfortunately, we are not attracting top cyber talent because morale is poor on the inside and the money is better on the outside.

I have proposed the creation of a stronger, consolidated cybersecurity agency at the Department of Homeland Security. This will help us step-up our cyber defense efforts and attract top talent.

And we have already begun to work with the Trump administration and others to make that a reality in the near future.

Finally, winning battles in cyber space depends on our ability to deliver consequences. As a former Federal prosecutor, I know that if you don't make the costs outweigh the benefits bad behavior will continue.

This requires strong leadership, a willingness to track down rogue hackers, and a determination to hold hostile countries accountable.

Chairman MCCAUL. With that, the Chair now recognizes the Ranking Member.

Mr. THOMPSON. Thank you, Mr. Chairman. I want to thank you for holding this hearing.

Cybersecurity is at the forefront of American politics in a way that in my 24 years here in Congress I have never seen before. On this committee we regularly gather to hear from cybersecurity leaders on the most pressing security vulnerabilities to our Nation and the novel ways enemies seek to exploit them.

This past fall details began to emerge about an entirely new attack vector—a hacking campaign designed to impact the Presidential election. Even before the election Secretary of Homeland Security Jeh Johnson and Director of National Intelligence James Clapper warned that Russian President Vladimir Putin directed hackers to penetrate the e-mail accounts of high-ranking Democratic officials to acquire information for the purpose of embarrassing and undermining the candidacy of Secretary Clinton.

We may never know whether the Russian intervention was the determining factor in such a close election. Still, Congress has a responsibility to address the unanimous determination of our intelligence community that Putin's government successfully meddled in our democracy and, in the view of the intelligence community, will do so again.

In fact, in response to a question about the risk of future Russian hacking against our election systems, FBI Director James Comey said, "They will be back."

The full scale of this state-sponsored hacking campaign is still not fully known, but what we do know is that in addition to hacking private e-mail accounts of prominent Democrats, the Russian hackers tried to infiltrate vital networks and equipment maintained by state election authorities. The Russian cyber campaign sought to strike at the heart of our democracy.

As such, legitimate questions about contacts between President Trump's inner circle and associates of the Putin regime need to be brought to light. That is why I support an independent, 9/11-style commission to investigate the Russian cyber campaign.

For our part, this committee needs to do aggressive oversight into this matter.

It is disheartening to see President Trump be dismissive about investigating this very significant cyber attack, even as DHS and its Federal partners work to raise the level of cyber awareness and hygiene across the country.

Just this week President Trump responded to the testimony from the FBI and NSA before the House Intelligence Committee that laid bare that there is no truth to the President's allegation that former President Obama tapped his wires—tweeted, "The Democrats made up and pushed the Russian story."

5

If this was all fake news then why would FBI Director Comey be dedicating scarce resources since July to investigating the Russian government's interference with our election and any links between individuals associated with the Trump campaign and the Russian government?

What seems to be lost on President Trump, who, during the campaign, repeatedly expressed support for DOD using cyber offensive capabilities, is that there can be no retribution without attribution.

I am pleased that we have with us today cybersecurity leaders who understand the dangers posed by state actors like Russia and who can speak to what we should be doing inside our Government and with our allies, including NATO, to protect critical infrastructure, including election infrastructure.

Before I yield back, Mr. Chair, I must express my deep concern also about the aloof—bordering on belligerent—posture taken by the Trump administration with respect to our NATO allies. Last week the President not only repeated an unsubstantiated Fox News claim that defamed the United Kingdom intelligence service, but when asked by German Chancellor Merkel to shake her hand at a White House press event, he refused.

This week we hear the Secretary of State will not be attending a long-scheduled NATO meeting, but plan to visit Russia in April. At this heightened threat to Europe, it is critical that this administration reverse course and reassure our NATO allies that we are full partners against all threats, but they and cyber or conventional threats also.

With that, Mr. Chair, I yield back.

[The statement of Ranking Member Thompson follows:]

STATEMENT OF RANKING MEMBER BENNIE G. THOMPSON

MARCH 22, 2017

Cybersecurity is at the forefront of American politics in a way that, in my 24 years in Congress, I have never seen.

On this committee, we regularly gather to hear from cybersecurity leaders on the most pressing security vulnerabilities to our Nation and the novel ways our enemies seek to exploit them.

This past fall, details began to emerge about an entirely new attack vector—a hacking campaign designed to impact the Presidential election.

Even before the election, Secretary of Homeland Security Jeh Johnson and Director of National Intelligence James Clapper warned that Russian President Vladimir Putin directed hackers to penetrate the email accounts of high-ranking Democratic officials to acquire information for the purpose of embarrassing and undermining the candidacy of Secretary Clinton.

We may never know whether the Russian intervention was the determining factor in such a close election. Still, Congress has a responsibility to address the unanimous determination of our intelligence community that Putin's government successfully meddled in our democracy and, in the view of the IC, will do so again.

In fact, in response to a question about the risk of future Russian hacking against our election systems, FBI Director James Comey said "they'll be back."

The full scale of this state-sponsored hacking campaign is still not fully known, but what we do know is that in addition to hacking private email accounts of prominent Democrats, the Russian hackers tried infiltrate vital networks and equipment maintained by state election authorities.

The Russian cyber campaign sought to strike at the heart of our democracy. As such, legitimate questions about contacts between President Trump's inner circle and associates of the Putin regime need to be brought to light.

That is why I support an independent 9/11-style commission to investigate the Russian cyber campaign. For our part, this committee needs to do aggressive oversight into this matter.

It is disheartening to see President Trump be dismissive about investigating this very significant cyber attack, even as DHS and its Federal partners work to raise the level of cyber awareness and hygiene across the country.

Just this week, President Trump, responding to testimony from the FBI and NSA before the House Intelligence Committee that laid bare that there is no truth to the President's allegations that former-President Obama "tapped his wires," tweeted "the Democrats made up and pushed the Russian story."

If this was all "fake news" then why would FBI Director Comey be dedicating scarce resources, since July, to investigating the Russian government's interference with our election and "any links between individuals associated with the Trump campaign and the Russian government"?

What seems to be lost on President Trump who, during the campaign, repeatedly expressed support for DoD using cyber offensive capabilities is that there can be no retribution without attribution.

I am pleased that we have with us today cybersecurity leaders who understand the dangers posed by state actors like Russia and can speak to what we should be doing inside our Government and with our allies, including NATO, to protect critical infrastructure, including election infrastructure.

Before I yield back, I must express my deep concern about the aloof, bordering on belligerent, posture taken by the Trump administration with respect to our NATO allies. Last week, the President not only repeated an unsubstantiated Fox News claim that defamed the U.K. intelligence service but, when asked by German Chancellor Merkel to shake her hand at a White House press event, refused.

This week, we hear that his Secretary of State will not be attending a long-scheduled NATO meeting but plans to visit Russia in April. At a time of heightened threat to Europe, it is critical that the Trump administration reverse course and reassure our NATO allies that we are full partners against all threats—be they cyber or conventional.

Chairman MCCAUL. Thank you, Ranking Member.

Other Members are reminded they may submit opening statements for the record.

We have a distinguished panel.

First, retired General Keith Alexander, president and CEO of the IronNet Cybersecurity. Prior to his work at IronNet the four-star general was the director of the National Security Agency.

Thank you, sir, for being here today.

Next we have Mr. Michael Daniel, president of the Cyber Threat Alliance, or CTA. Before that he served as special assistant to the president and cybersecurity coordinator on the National Security Council staff.

Thank you, sir, as well.

Mr. Frank Cilluffo is the director of the Center for Cyber and Homeland Security at the George Washington University and is co-director of G.W.'s Cyber Center for National and Economic Security.

Thank you, sir.

Finally, Mr. Bruce McConnell is the global vice president of the EastWest Institute. Prior to joining the institute he served as deputy under secretary for cybersecurity at the U.S. Department of Homeland Security.

Thank you, sir.

I want to thank all of you for being here.

I now recognize General Alexander.

STATEMENT OF GENERAL KEITH B. ALEXANDER (RET. USA), PRESIDENT AND CHIEF EXECUTIVE OFFICER, IRONNET CYBERSECURITY

General ALEXANDER. Chairman McCaul, Ranking Member Thompson, distinguished Members of the committee, it is an honor to be here.

Chairman McCaul, I am going to take from some of your statements and walk through my thoughts on the threat, where I think we need to go as a Nation, and specifically with respect to the Department of Homeland Security in the next 4 hours—no, I am going to take my 5 minutes.

So you are right, the threats out there are growing, Chairman, as we see them. You see it from Russia. It has hit our elections; it has hit a number of areas.

We see this around the world with Iran on Saudi Arabia, most disturbing and the ones that concern me the most. You have seen North Korea on Sony and others. It is growing.

I think there are two aspects of this that we need to address. First, our defense is terrible—between Government and industry, and with industry getting the information they need from Government, and the coordination within Government. It has to be better.

You know, it was interesting being on the Presidential commission. One of the things that we recognized is people said it is too hard to do A, B, C, or D, but when you look at our Constitution it says "for the common defense." It doesn't have in parentheses, "unless it is too hard."

It says it is for the common defense. That is what we have our Government for.

Actually, we can defend this Nation in cybersecurity working with industry. Actually, what Mr. Daniel is doing with Cyber Threat Alliance, and what Homeland Security is doing, and what the rest of the Government is doing sets the pieces in place.

We have got to force that together. Let me give you some thoughts on how to do that.

When we talk about this bubble chart that you mentioned about how we got the agencies together, it gave clear—fairly clear—missions to the Defense Department, to the Department of Justice, FBI, and to Homeland Security. But words matter, and what I see in those words is there is a lot of confusion over the difference in some of the words.

So what do you mean by "protect" and what do you mean by "defend"? Whose responsibility is it, and how are we going to work together?

It is clear that if we work together—and industry sees this. You see the financial sector starting to work together; they are passing things through the FS–ISAC. You see the energy sector and all the other sectors doing that, in large part led by some of the DHS efforts on critical infrastructure.

That is a step in the right direction.

What Mr. Daniel is working on is a cyber threat alliance, sharing information. What we have got to get to is how we share information within Government and with industry at network speed so that when this Nation is attacked all the elements of our Government are prepared to do their job, which I would tell you from my perspective today, we are not prepared.

We need to up that defense. We need to share information so that DHS can do the job that I believe it is there for, which, as you noted in yours, it is not the Defense Department or the intelligence community's job to police domestic networks—nor, actually, is it any Government—but they have to get information from them when they are being attacked.

I will use Sony as a case in point. Let's say that we determined that Sony was critical infrastructure—I will leave that to someone else. But if Sony is being attacked by a nation-state, whose job is it to defend Sony if we will not allow Sony to counter-attack?

That is the Government's job, in my opinion.

But the Government did not and could not see that attack. We didn't have the information at network speed; we had not practiced it; and as you said, Chairman, we don't have the rules of engagement and we haven't set this up.

We need to fix that now.

First, industry, from my perspective, is more than willing to share. It is not personally identifiable information; it is threat information, and we can share that at network speed. If industry can share it amongst companies within a sector, they could also share that with the Government.

We agreed early on that that would go through DHS but should be shared to the rest of Government so those that have a responsibility—whether it is law enforcement—for defense of the country could do their job at network speed. I know you have pushed hard on that, Chairman, to make sure that that is right. We should ensure that is right and practice that.

If we did that, when Sony is being attacked by North Korea in that case, and if the President and the Secretary of Defense determine a cyber response was valid, they would have the means and wherewithal to do a cyber response before we lost Sony.

Companies don't want the Government there for incident response. They want us there when they are being defended. They don't want to end up to be a victim like Sony, and we can't afford that in many of our sectors, so we have to get this right.

Chairman, I am prepared to answer any questions that you have. Thank you very much.

[The prepared statement of General Alexander follows:]

PREPARED STATEMENT OF KEITH B. ALEXANDER

MARCH 22, 2017

Chairman McCaul, Ranking Member Thompson, Members of the committee: Thank you for inviting me to discuss Defending Against Cyber Threats with you today, and specifically, the current cyber threat landscape, civilian cyber defense capabilities, and deterrence. I plan to speak candidly about the authorities, roles, and responsibilities of the Federal Government in cyber space, and how we can provide for our Nation's common defense in cyber space. While some see the offense as superior to the defense when it comes to cybersecurity, I believe that these need to be worked together between the Government and industry.

I want to thank both Chairman McCaul and Ranking Member Thompson for making cybersecurity a top priority, including your bipartisan efforts to develop much of the legislation at the heart of the Cybersecurity Act of 2015 and earlier legislation that set the stage for it. This includes the efforts to codify and strengthen the authorities related to the National Cybersecurity and Communications Integration

Center (NCCIC) and to improve Federal cyber defense efforts, including positive changes to the Federal Information Security Management Act (FISMA) and provisions that will make it easier for us to grow a more capable Federal cyber workforce.

We live in an age in which data, and access to data, are key resources. Never has technology been so focused on how we create, use, and communicate data, and this revolution will benefit us as it leads the way for significant strides in technology. It was just over 10 years ago that Apple introduced the first iPhone, a portable communications device with a faster processor, more memory, and more storage space than the Cray supercomputers of the 1980's and 1990's. In the same year the iPhone was introduced, we witnessed cyber attacks being used as an element of National power in the attacks on Estonia, the most digitally dependent country in the world. Ten years later, we continue to witness an astounding rate of growth in the amount of unique, new information available world-wide, not to mention huge increases in the velocity of data being transmitted and types of devices communicating information. With the birth of the Internet of Things (IoT) and the continued development and rapid iteration of technology, these trends are likely to continue to accelerate.

We have also witnessed a troubling change in cyber attacks, including an increase in major disruptive attacks, as well as the use of actual destructive attacks on both public and private-sector entities in the United States and abroad. In 2012, we saw the advent of destructive attacks against Saudi Aramco, with over 20,000 computers affected, and a follow-on attack against Qatari RasGas.[1] Similar attacks have recently been reported against the Saudi government.[2] Here in the United States, we have seen destructive attacks conducted by nation-states against private institutions, including the Las Vegas Sands Corporation and Sony Corporation.[3] We have likewise seen massive disruptive attacks targeting American financial institutions, including major attacks taking place multiple times in the last 5 years. Most recently, we have seen what appear to be cyber-enabled efforts targeting the election of the President of the United States.

We have also seen massive data breaches targeting nearly every major economic sector here in the United States, perhaps most prominently in the customer facing sides of key retailers and health insurers. We have likewise seen an increasing trend with respect to the use of ransomware by organized criminal groups and small actors alike, seeking to hold data or systems hostage at a range of organizations across our Nation, from hospitals to educational institutions. According to one report, the key sectors affected by ransomware include the services and manufacturing sectors, making up a combined 55% of ransomware infections.[4]

This does not even account for the on-going theft of intellectual property from American companies, which I believe continues to represent the greatest transfer of wealth in human history. While we have ostensibly seen a significant down tick in cyber-enabled intellectual property theft by key nation-state actors, it remains to be seen whether this change will be sustained in the long-run and whether it represents an actual reduction in significant activity versus simply a more refined focus on key high-value theft.[5]

---

[1] See Director of National Intelligence James R. Clapper, Statement for the Record: *Worldwide Threat Assessment of the U.S. Intelligence Community 2013* at 1, Senate Select Committee on Intelligence (Mar. 12, 2013), available on-line at *https://www.dni.gov/files/documents/Intelligence%20Reports/2013%20ATA%20SFR%20for%20SSCI%2012%20Mar%202013.pdf*; Kim Zetter, *Qatari Gas Company Hit With Virus in Wave of Attacks on Energy Companies* (Aug. 30, 2012), available on-line at *https://www.wired.com/2012/08/hack-attack-strikes-rasgas/*.

[2] See Zahraa Alkhalisi, *Saudi Arabia Warns of New Crippling Cyberattack*, CNN (Jan. 26, 2017), available on-line at *http://money.cnn.com/2017/01/25/technology/saudi-arabia-cyberattack-warning/*; see also Jose Pagliery, *Hackers Destroy Computers at Saudi Aviation Agency*, CNN (Dec. 2, 2016) available on-line at *http://money.cnn.com/2016/12/01/technology/saudi-arabia-hack-shamoon/?iid=EL*.

[3] See Director of National Intelligence James R. Clapper, Opening Statement to *Worldwide Threat Assessment Hearing*, Senate Armed Services Committee (Feb. 26, 2015), available on-line at *https://www.dni.gov/files/documents/2015%20WWTA%20As%20Delivered%20DNI%20-Oral%20Statement.pdf* ("2014 saw, for the first-time, destructive cyber attacks carried out on U.S. soil by nation-state entities, marked first by the Iranian attack on the Las Vegas Sands Casino a year ago this month and the North Korean attack against Sony in November. Although both of these nations have lesser technical capabilities in comparison to Russia and China, these destructive attacks demonstrate that Iran and North Korea are motivated and unpredictable cyber actors.").

[4] See Symantec, *An ISTR Report: Ransomware and Businesses 2016*, at 8, available on-line at *http://www.symantec.com/content/en/us/enterprise/media/security_response/whitepapers/ISTR2016_Ransomware_and_Businesses.pdf*.

[5] See Federal News Service, Transcript: *Hearing Before the Senate Armed Services Committee on Cybersecurity Policy and Threats* at 8 (Sept. 29, 2015) ("McCain: As a result of the Chinese

Continued

And it is worth noting that the same network penetrations that permit threat actors to steal data can potentially be used to disrupt networks or destroy data. This is particularly important to understand as we watch the increasing convergence of our systems and networks, whether we are talking about the increased links between industrial control systems and corporate networks or the proliferation of devices that are connected to the global network as part of the expansion of the IoT.

We recently saw the practical implications of broad connectivity and convergence when the Mirai botnet turned run-of-the-mill devices into a virtual IoT army and used them to execute a Distributed Denial of Service (DDoS) attack on Dyn (recently acquired by Oracle), a managed DNS and traffic optimization company that serves more than 3,500 enterprise customers, including major companies like Netflix, Twitter, LinkedIn, and CNBC.[6]

As a free society, we have many vulnerabilities and leave ourselves open to various threats that more authoritarian nations are more capable of combating by limiting access to resources or restricting the freedom of their people. Here in the United States, we are most vulnerable to two asymmetric threats: Terrorist attacks and cyber-enabled attacks. While these two types of attacks may overlap, and terrorist groups seek to obtain such capabilities, today the most advanced capabilities are in the hands of nation-states. This is not to discount the threat posed by criminal actors; To the contrary, the most wide-spread threat to our people today comes from organized criminal groups employing cyber-enabled capabilities to make money.

It is worth noting that our enemies today need not attack our Government to have a substantive strategic effect on our Nation. Attacking civilian or economic infrastructure may be a more effective approach in the modern era, particularly for asymmetric actors like terrorist groups. Our increasing reliance on digital, connected devices means that while tanks, bombers, and fighter jets are certainly not obsolete, there are newer and perhaps more insidious ways of having similar effects without the need for the large investment that those assets require. Nation-states have long sought access to the critical systems of other nations for espionage, and we now see an expansion from these traditional activities to more aggressive actions by nation-states. The number of nations that possess the capability to exploit and attack continues to grow with less of an incentive to act with appropriate state-to-state behavior and the using these cyber capabilities in a more aggressive way.

Similarly, an increasing number and range of non-state groups use cyber-enabled methods to advance their own agendas. Major criminal gangs, organized crime groups, and terrorist organizations are growing their cyber capabilities to go beyond mere communication, recruitment, and incitement. And though the RAND Corporation estimates that the malware black market can be more profitable than the illegal drug trade,[7] we do not treat cyber space threats as an epidemic. Nor do we treat nation-state threats, or worse, nation-state actions, in cyber space as we would treat the presence of nation-states key naval assets inside our territorial waters. Rather, we treat cyber threats largely as nuisance or, at worst, criminal activity to be dealt with principally through private-sector defensive measures and after-the-fact government action, typically by traditional law enforcement agencies. The future of warfare is here, and we need to structure and architect our Nation to defend our country in cyber space.

It is critical that as a Nation, we fundamentally rethink how the Government and the private sector relate to one another in cyber space. We need to draw clear lines and make explicit certain responsibilities, capabilities, and authorities. The private sector controls the vast majority of the real estate in cyber space, particularly when it comes to critical infrastructure and key resources.[8] Given the private sector's role in running the infrastructure upon which our Nation relies, there is likewise no question that the Government and private sector must collaborate. We need to rec-

---

leader in Washington there was some agreement announced between the United States and China. Do you believe that that will result in an elimination of Chinese cyber attacks? Clapper: Well, hope springs eternal. I think we will have to watch what they're behavior is and it will be incumbent on the intelligence community I think to depict, portray to policymakers what behavioral changes if any, result from this agreement. McCain: Are you optimistic? Clapper: No.").

[6] See Dyn, About Dyn, available on-line at *http://dyn.com/about/*.

[7] See Lillian Ablon, Martin C. Libicki, and Andrea A. Golay, *Markets for Cybercrime Tools and Stolen Data* at 11, RAND Corporation (2014), available on line at *http://www.rand.org/pubs/research_reports/RR610.html*.

[8] See, e.g., Office of the Director of National Intelligence, Office of the Program Manager-Information Sharing Environment, *Critical Infrastructure and Key Resources*, available on-line at *https://www.ise.gov/missionpartners/critical-infrastructure-and-key-resources* ("The private sector owns and operates an estimated 85% of infrastructure and resources critical to our Nation's physical and economic security.").

ognize that neither the Government nor the private sector can capably protect the systems and networks they need to without extensive and close cooperation.

One of the key issues we must address is determining where to place responsibility for the cyber defense of the Nation, including its key infrastructures and economic sectors. Today, the basic expectation is that the private sector is responsible for defending itself in cyber space regardless of the enemy, scale of attack, or type of capabilities employed. However, the reality is that commercial, private-sector entities cannot practically be expected to defend themselves against nation-state attacks in cyber space. They do not have the capacity or capability to respond in a way that would be fully effective against a nation-state attacker, whether from a deterrence or strategic perspective.

For over 200 years, our Constitution has made clear that one of the core goals of our forefathers in forming a Federal union was to provide "for the common defense."[9] And yet today, as we face a rapidly expanding threat environment in cyber space and as our National institutions and our economic base in the private sector increasingly come under direct attack from a wide range of actors including highly capable nation-states, we simply do not provide such common defense, at least not in any practical sense of the phrase.

In 2012, then-Secretary of Defense Leon Panetta noted that "the Department [of Defense] has a responsibility . . . to be prepared to defend the Nation and our National interests against an attack in or through cyber space."[10] Even at that time, it was clear that in order to make our overall national cyber architecture truly defensible, we needed to establish a shared understanding of our respective roles and responsibilities, first within the Government, then between the Government and the private sector. As a result, we worked closely with our colleagues in other agencies across the Government spending many hours, days, weeks, and months to put in place a workable structure for sharing authorities and assigning responsibilities at the National level. Indeed, by one count, it took 75 drafts to get agreement on a single slide regarding the National division of responsibilities for cybersecurity.[11]

At the end of that process, we assigned the responsibilities as follows: The Justice Department would, among other things, "[i]nvestigate, attribute, disrupt, and prosecute cyber crimes; [l]ead domestic national security operations; and [c]onduct domestic collection, analysis, and dissemination of cyber threat intelligence;" DHS would "[c]oordinate the national protection, prevention, mitigation of, and recovery from cyber incidents; [d]isseminate domestic cyber threat and vulnerability analysis; and [p]rotect critical infrastructure;" and DOD would "[d]efend the Nation from attack; [g]ather foreign threat intelligence and determine attribution; [s]ecure national security and military systems."[12] Moreover, the "bubble chart," as this document was called, assigned the following lead roles: DOJ: investigation and enforcement; DHS: protection; and DOD: National defense.[13]

The reality, however, is that the vision of the "bubble chart" has never been fully realized. The truth is that today, our Government agencies appear to be confused by the different terms of protection, incident response, and National defense. More needs to be done in defining these roles within the key departments, and we must practice how the Government is going to collectively execute their responsibilities. The relationships amongst our various Government agencies and between the Government and the private sector continue to be a source of friction, the "bubble chart" notwithstanding. Clearly more remains to be done to fully achieve the valuable vision set forth in the "bubble chart."

Many have also argued that it is important for the creation of "a new component agency, or [the] repurpose[ing of] an existing agency, to serve as a fully operational cybersecurity and critical infrastructure protection agency on par with other compo-

---

[9] U.S. Const., preamble (emphasis added and spelling modernized).

[10] See Department of Defense, Remarks by Secretary Panetta on Cybersecurity to the Business Executives for National Security, New York City (Oct. 11, 2012), available on-line at *http://archive.defense.gov/transcripts/transcript.aspx?transcriptid=5136.*

[11] See Department of Defense Information Operations Center for Research and Army Reserve Cyber Operations Group, Cyber Endeavor 2014: Final Report—When the Lights Go Out, at 5 (June 26, 2014), available on-line at *https://my.nps.edu/documents/105372694/0/ Cyber_Endeavour_2014-Final_Report-2014-08-13.pdf.* ("The need to define these partnerships and relationships [] led the Government and U.S. Federal Cybersecurity Operations Team to define their National roles and relationships as highlighted in Figure 1, which is commonly referred to as the 'Bubble Chart.' There were seventy-five (75) versions made of this chart before all parties agreed on how this works, and it was powerful and important just to get an agreement.")

[12] See id. at 6, Fig. 1.

[13] See id.

nent agencies."[14] This agency would be a "DISA equivalent" for the civilian Government agencies. This could be run by the Government or outsourced to a commercial entity. As I've previously noted, I generally support this recommendation, and think that it is important that the new administration give this idea some serious consideration.

For the Government to effectively work with the private sector to secure the Nation in cyber space, perhaps the single most important thing the Government can do is to build real connectivity and interoperability with the private sector. Such connectivity and interoperability on a technology level is critical, but it is also important on the policy and governance level. That is, in part why the Commission recommended the creation of a National Cybersecurity Public-Private Partnership (NCP³).[15] This entity, as set forth in Commission's report, would serve the President directly, reporting directly through the National Security Advisor and would be used "as a forum for addressing cybersecurity issues through a high-level, joint public-private collaboration."[16] Part of the NCP³'s key role would be to "identify clear roles and responsibilities for the private and public sectors in defending the Nation in cyber space," including addressing critical issues like "attribution, sharing of Classified information [and] an approach—including recommendations on the authorities and rules of engagement needed—to enable cooperative efforts between the Government and private sector to protect the Nation, including cooperative operations, training, and exercises."

In line with this recommendation, the Commission also recommended that the "[t]he private sector and administration should launch a joint cybersecurity operation program for the public and private sectors to collaborate on cybersecurity activities to identify, protect from, detect, respond to, and recover from cyber incidents affecting critical infrastructure."[17] In my view, empowering such joint efforts is critical to ensuring our long-term National security in cyber space. As the Commission indicated, "[k]ey aspects of any collaborative defensive effort between the Government and private sector [will] include coordinated protection and detection approaches to ensure resilience; fully integrated response, recovery, and plans; a series of annual cooperative training programs and exercises coordinated with key agencies and industry; and the development of interoperable systems."[18] Having such mechanisms in place well ahead of crisis is critical so that public and private sector entities can jointly train and exercise these rules of engagement and mitigate any potential spillover effects on on-going business or Government activities. In my view, implementing these two recommendations of the Commission are amongst the most important things we might do as a Nation in the near term.

Finally, I think it is worth highlighting that it is critical that this be a two-way partnership between Government and the private sector. The Government can and must do more when it comes to partnering with the private sector, building trust, and sharing threat information—yes, even highly Classified threat information—at network speed and in a form that can be actioned rapidly. Building out a cross-cutting information-sharing capability allows the Government and private sector to develop a common operating picture, analogous to the air traffic control picture. As the air traffic control picture ensures our aviation safety and synchronizes Government and civil aviation, the cyber common operational picture can be used to synchronize a common cyber defense for our Nation, drive decision making, and enable rapid response across our entire National cyber infrastructure. This would prove a critical defensive capability for the Nation.

The information-sharing legislation enacted by Congress as part of the Cybersecurity Act of 2015 is a step in the right direction. However, it lacks key features to truly encourage robust sharing, including placing overbearing requirements on the private sector, overly limiting liability protections, restricting how information might effectively be shared with the Government, and keeping the specter of potential Government regulation looming in the background.[19] Moreover, while the Government has placed this responsibility with the DHS today,[20] and DHS established

---

[14] Id. at 44 (action item 5.5.2).

[15] Id. at 14 (action item 1.2.1).

[16] Id. at 14–15.

[17] Id. at 15 (action item 1.2.2.)

[18] Id.

[19] See, e.g., Jamil N. Jaffer, *Carrots and Sticks in Cyberspace: Addressing Key Issues in the Cybersecurity Information Sharing Act of 2015*, S. Car. L. Rev. (forthcoming 2017).

[20] See, e.g., Executive Order 13691, *Promoting Private Sector Cybersecurity Information Sharing* (Feb. 13, 2015),available on-line at *https://www.whitehouse.gov/the-press-office/2015/02/13/executive-order-promoting-private-sector-cybersecurity-information-shari* ("The National Cybersecurity and Communications Integration Center (NCCIC), established under section 226(b) of the Homeland Security Act of 2002 . . . shall engage in continuous, collaborative, and inclu-

the Automated Indicator Sharing platform (AIS) as a "capability [that] enables the exchange of cyber threat indicators between the Federal Government and the private sector at machine speed,"[21] it is important for this Committee—as the primary oversight organization for the Department—to recognize the perception in industry is that DHS faces significant challenges in this area and that it simply lacks the technical capabilities to succeed.[22] When we first discussed this approach, DHS was the portal, but it would be a true partnership between DOD, DHS, and DOJ. We must help drive DOD, DHS, and DOJ to work together to evolve our Government's roles and responsibilities.

More can be done here, and I stand ready to work with this committee and others in Congress and the administration as we seek a path forward on this important issue. As with the recommendations of the Commission above, I believe that implementing real, robust real-time threat information sharing across the private sector and with the Government could be a game-changer when it comes to cyber defense.

In sum, Mr. Chairman, I think much remains to be done to fully put our Nation on a path to real security in cyber space, but I am strongly hopeful for our future. With your leadership and that of the Ranking Member, working together collaboratively across the aisle and with the White House and key players in the private sector as well as other key committees in Congress, I think we can achieve some real successes in the near future.

Chairman MCCAUL. Thank you, General.
Chair recognizes Mr. Daniel.

STATEMENT OF MICHAEL DANIEL, PRESIDENT, CYBER THREAT ALLIANCE

Mr. DANIEL. Thank you, Mr. Chairman, Ranking Member Thompson, other distinguished committee Members. It is very nice to be here with you today with such a distinguished panel.

I want to build on what General Alexander was saying in terms of how I see the threat evolving and talk briefly about why this problem is actually hard, because it is not obvious on the surface of it, and then talk a little bit about how we have some strategies for dealing with it and how CTA can play a role in that.

When you take a look at the threat space that we are talking about you can see three trends that make it—that make this problem continue to get worse, one of which is that we are making it broader. Every day we are hooking up more and more stuff to the internet, and we are hooking up different kinds of items.

It is no longer just wired desktops but, you know, refrigerators and cars and light bulbs and a whole array of medical devices and other things that are very, very different from one another. So we are making our problem continually more difficult.

It is also becoming—the threat is also becoming more diverse. Many different actors are learning that they can pursue their interests through cyber space, whether they are hacktivists or criminals or nation-states, and all of those factors mean that the problem is becoming along a much greater continuum than it was before.

sive coordination with ISAOs on the sharing of information related to cybersecurity risks and incidents.").

[21] See DHS US–CERT, Automated Indicator Sharing (AIS), available on-line at *https:// www.us-cert.gov/ais.*

[22] See Commission on Enhancing National Cybersecurity, Testimony of Greg Rattray, Director of Global Cyber Partnerships & Government Strategy, J.P. Morgan Chase (May 16, 2016) (describing DHS's six information sharing initiatives, as "too broad and [simply] not meet[ing] the need [] to enhance cyber defense"); Testimony of Mark Gordon, n. 13 supra (arguing that while tactically accelerating automating and systemizing threat indicator content with the Government is a big vision, it is not a reality today); see also Jaffer, n. 14 supra, at__ ("DHS is generally seen as facing major challenges in capability in the cyber area and a number of other agencies, from DOD/NSA to FBI, are seen by industry as more capable, reliable, or secure.").

It is becoming more dangerous. People are willing to take actions in cyber space and cause disruption and destruction in a way that they weren't previously.

Now, it is not obvious on the surface why this problem is actually hard to deal with, but I think it is because we tend to treat it as just a technology problem and we keep trying to impose just technology solutions on this problem. It is not just a technology problem.

It involves aspects of economics, and human behavior, business issues, political issues. Until we learn to address it in that holistic manner and not continue to treat it just as a technology problem, we are going to continue to fail, as General Alexander was saying.

But it is also because cyber space has some different rules. It doesn't operate the way the physical world does.

Certain concepts like near and far, proximity, sovereignty—all of these things actually have different meanings in cyber space than they do in the way they manifest in the physical world. So we have got to learn to grapple with the different rules that cyber space imposes on us.

Last, this is just a new policy area. We don't have centuries of experience, decades of a policy framework to draw on. Almost everything that we are doing in this space—the bubble chart that General Alexander referenced—that is all new, and figuring out how to do this is a challenge.

I think overall when I look at where we are trying to get to, information sharing is obviously a critical enabler. I would say that it is a necessary but not sufficient part of what we need to do in terms of our defense.

We have talked about it for a long time. In fact, there are those that are sort-of tired of talking about information sharing. Frank is probably one of them. Part of the issue is that we actually haven't figured out how to do it right.

We have taken some really good steps. The legislation that this committee helped pass and get through was a critical part of that, some of the Executive Orders from the previous administration, some of the steps in the private sector. But we really haven't gotten to the point where we are doing it at network speed and at scale.

So I see the model that we are trying with the Cyber Threat Alliance of bringing together the cybersecurity industry in a new way, using some new models of how to share that information, score that information, give that information some value, emphasize context, not just the raw data itself—if we begin to pool this information in a way—in this new way we will actually enable the cybersecurity vendors to raise their defenses across the entire ecosystem.

But it will also enable us to work with Government better to actually disrupt what the bad guys are doing and actually change the dynamic from always being on the defense to actually being able to take the fight to the bad guys. It will enable us to do better analysis so we can take that risk-based approach that the NIST Cybersecurity Framework promotes, and so that companies can actually implement that much more effectively. It will make our response and recovery activities much more effective because it will be based on solid data.

So just to close, you know, this is an area that I agree with what you said, Mr. Chairman, that this is an absolutely critical problem for us to tackle, and I am very committed from both my Government service and in my current role to doing so. So thank you very much.

[The prepared statement of Mr. Daniel follows:]

PREPARED STATEMENT OF MICHAEL DANIEL

MARCH 22, 2017

Chairman McCaul, Ranking Member Thompson and Members of the committee: Thank you for the opportunity to appear before you today to discuss how new models of collaboration and threat sharing can be a catalyst toward tangibly reducing threats across the cybersecurity ecosystem. My name is Michael Daniel and, as of last Monday, I am the first president of the Cyber Threat Alliance (CTA)—a cyber threat information-sharing organization that now includes six of the world's largest cybersecurity companies as founding members. Prior to leading the CTA, I served for over 20 years in the U.S. Federal Government, most recently for 4 years as Special Assistant to the President and Cybersecurity Coordinator at the National Security Council.

First, let me begin my testimony by acknowledging this committee's longstanding leadership on cybersecurity issues. This committee has played a central role in passing a range of important cybersecurity legislation, including legislation that has helped foster a more robust and trusted environment for responsible cyber threat information sharing. Having worked on cyber threat information-sharing issues first-hand for many years, I understand how challenging this process was and sincerely appreciate this committee's continued hard work and leadership.

THE CYBER THREAT LANDSCAPE

We live in a digital age. This digital age brings with it incredible efficiencies and productivity, but it also brings new challenges and potential vulnerabilities that— left unchecked—threaten to undermine these very benefits. The increasingly digitized nature of the world, and the United States in particular, means the threats we face in cyber space are particularly significant. Our economy, our National security, our social lives all depend heavily on the internet and cyber space. Unfortunately, the threat is also growing more acute in at least three fundamental ways:

1. The cyber threat is becoming broader: As we increasingly connect more and more devices up to the internet, we are making cyber space bigger and dramatically expanding the potential attack surface. Indeed, even by the Gartner Group's conservative estimates, there will be over 20 billion devices connected to the internet by 2020—that translates to adding 10 million devices per day. But more important than just the numbers are the kind of devices we are connecting to the internet. They are not desktops, laptops, or even smartphones. They are light bulbs, refrigerators, cars, thermostats, sensors, and thousands of other "things"—a huge array of different kinds of devices with different functions, protocols, and security features. This growth in volume and heterogeneity makes effective cyber defense even harder.

2. The cyber threat is becoming more frequent: The number of malicious actors in cyber space continues to grow rapidly as hacktivists, criminals, and nation-states all learn that they can pursue their goals relatively cheaply and effectively through cyber space. The barriers to entry are low and the potential return on investment is fairly high. As a result, the volume and frequency of malicious cyber activity is increasing dramatically.

3. The cyber threat is becoming more dangerous: Until recently, cyber actors generally limited their malicious activities to stealing money or information, temporary denial-of-service attacks, or website defacements (the digital equivalent of graffiti). But increasingly, we are now seeing actors move to much more destructive and disruptive activities. The destructive cyber attack on Sony Pictures Entertainment, the physical disruption of the Ukrainian power grid, and the use of information operations to influence electoral processes are all recent examples of this trend.

WHY IS CYBERSECURITY A HARD CHALLENGE TO SOLVE?

At first glance, it's not obvious why cyber threats are so hard to effectively manage. If it's just a technology problem, why can't we simply deploy innovative technical solutions to stop these threats? The answer is that cyber threats pose not just technical problems, but also economic, psychological, and human behavioral challenges. As a result, our response to threats has to involve not just technical solutions, but economic, psychological, and human behavioral aspects as well—a much greater challenge than simply buying a new cybersecurity device or service.

In addition, cyber space operates according to different rules than the physical world. I do not mean the social "rules" of cyber space that get a lot of play in the media, but rather the physics and math of cyber space. The concepts of distance, borders, proximity—all operate differently in cyber space compared to the physical world. Therefore, our typical models for addressing certain challenges, such as border security, simply don't work in cyber space. Developing these new models will take time and experimentation to get right.

Finally, cyber space and the internet are still very new, relatively speaking. From a policy and legal perspective, we have not had the time or the experience to develop the comprehensive frameworks we need to tackle cybersecurity's challenges. What is the right division of responsibility between governments and the private sector in terms of cyber defense? What actions are acceptable for governments, companies, and individuals to take and which actions are not? Answering these kinds of questions is the fundamental policy challenge for the next few years.

WHAT SHOULD WE DO ABOUT CYBERSECURITY?

Given the trends, growing complexities, and inherent challenges of the cyber threat, is it possible to design an effective strategy to combat it? The short answer is yes—but implementing such a strategy requires a lot of work, sustained engagement, and a multi-disciplinary, risk-based approach. As a Nation, an effective cyber strategy will involve three core elements:
- Raising the level of cybersecurity across the global digital ecosystem
- Preventing, disrupting, deterring, and constraining our adversaries' operations in cyber space
- Responding effectively to incidents when they occur

From an organizational perspective, an effective cyber strategy must also contain several core elements:
- Making cybersecurity a C-suite and organizational priority
- Using a risk-based approach to address cyber threats
- Developing, testing, and exercising an incident response and recovery plan

In developing their strategies to combat cyber threats, governments should recognize that no one agency has the full range of capabilities, authorities, and perspective needed to address the challenge. Organizations must realize that they cannot relegate cybersecurity to the Chief Information Officer's (CIO) shop or the geeks in the server closet. Collectively, we must realize no government or individual company can effectively address the cyber threat by itself. Instead, cybersecurity is a fundamentally shared and distributed challenge that can only be effectively addressed through collaboration that leverages the unique capabilities and authorities of companies, individuals, and governments. The private sector, State and local governments, National governments—all of these entities will have to work together across boundaries and borders if we want our cybersecurity strategies to be effective.

In considering how to build this new kind of collaboration, I don't have "the" solution for what it should look like. In fact, there's almost certainly not just one solution. However, through the hard work of many people over the past decade and a half, we have started building the foundations for this new kind of collaboration. This committee has passed critical legislation that enables this collaboration within the U.S. The Federal Government has worked hard to build its capabilities across all the relevant agencies—Homeland Security, Defense, Commerce, State, Justice, GSA, OMB, and the intelligence community all have critical roles to play within the U.S. context. This kind of interagency collaboration will be necessary in other countries as well. The private sector has also been working hard globally, creating new structures, like Information Sharing and Analysis Organizations, building new technologies, and creating whole new industries, like cyber incident response firms. So the good news is that we do not need to start over. Instead, we can continue building on this foundation laid over the last decade to evolve this collaboration into its effective form.

CYBER THREAT INFORMATION SHARING AS A CRITICAL COMPONENT OF EFFECTIVE
CYBERSECURITY

Clearly, if we are going to have the kind of interagency, intercompany, and inter-organizational collaboration I described above, cyber threat information sharing is a critical enabler. In fact, robust cyber threat information sharing across this entire cybersecurity ecosystem is a necessity in achieving our shared goals of enhanced cybersecurity. Of course, cyber threat information sharing won't solve the problem by itself. If it is not used as a tool to leverage people, process, and technology to match the highly automated nature of our adversaries' attacks with automated defenses, then it will not be effective.

Despite this obvious enabling function, as a society we've had trouble figuring out how to actually share useful cyber threat information, do so at a speed that matters, and then to take action based on that information. That's where the CTA comes in.

HOW DOES CTA HELP ACHIEVE THESE GOALS OF AUTOMATED DEFENSE?

Within the cyber threat information-sharing environment, cybersecurity companies have a unique role to play. They collectively have the physical infrastructure and processing ability to automatically deploy preventive measures based on new cyber threat information to a broad customer base across multiple sectors. For these reasons, cybersecurity companies can bring a degree of "actionability" to cyber threat information sharing that is critical for achieving the ultimate goal of raising adversary costs and tangibly improving cybersecurity across the ecosystem.

To make this potential real, a core group of cybersecurity companies decided to form the Cyber Threat Alliance (CTA). CTA is a new kind of Information Sharing and Analysis Organization (ISAO) that features six of the largest global cybersecurity companies as founding members—Check Point, Cisco, Fortinet, McAfee, Palo Alto Networks and Symantec. It also includes IntSights, Rapid7, Reversing Labs, RSA, and Telefonica as affiliate members. This partnership underscores the philosophy that we can be force multipliers in support of a coordinated cyber threat information-sharing effort against our shared cyber adversaries. The CTA cyber threat information-sharing model is novel in several ways that directly address many of the aspects that have limited the effectiveness of other cyber threat information-sharing relationships, both formal and informal:

1. *Accountability.*—The CTA ensures that there is no anonymity for member contributions, although the customer's data is anonymized. Therefore, submitters have to stand behind the accuracy of the cyber threat information they provide.

2. *Participation.*—To encourage active participation and meaningful contributions, the CTA establishes mandatory submission thresholds for cyber threat information sharing, initially on a quantitative basis in an ever-evolving scoring system that measures the qualitative value of shared cyber threat data based on context.

3. *Transparency.*—The CTA uses an automated scoring algorithm to evaluate and assign point totals of submitted cyber threat intelligence that will be public among all members. CTA members will all be able to measure their performance on a dashboard.

Using this new cyber threat-sharing model, CTA undertakes two broad operational lines of effort. First, CTA enables near-real time sharing of rich, contextual cyber threat information among all cybersecurity companies, which can be leveraged on an individual basis to update and improve their products and services. Second, CTA uses this shared cyber threat information to build "playbooks" of malicious cyber activity. Taken together, these two broad lines of effort enable CTA to support both National and organizational cybersecurity objectives, including:

1. *Improved cyber defense across the entire ecosystem.*—By enabling cybersecurity providers to dramatically expand the pool of information their defensive products can leverage, every member's products become more effective for their customers. Because the CTA members' customers span all industry sectors, the impact of this cyber threat information sharing can protect a larger percentage of the global ecosystem than more sector-specific information sharing entities.

2. *Better prevention against, and disruption of our adversaries.*—The CTA is focused on sharing indicators related to an adversary's playbook—a more limited and predictable series of steps an adversary must take to complete a successful cyber attack. Although re-engineering malware requires some time and effort, relatively speaking it is easy to make small tweaks to malware so that it can evade detection. However, an adversaries' total suite of indicators (the "playbook," including tactics, techniques, and procedures, and typical operational approach) is much more difficult to change and update. By developing and pub-

lishing these playbooks, we can force adversaries to adapt their business processes—a much more time consuming and therefore disruptive task.

3. Risk-based.—As CTA's cyber threat information base grows, it will enable better analysis of cyber threats and trends with respect to those threats.—In turn, this analysis will enable our members to better advise clients on the relative risks of the cyber threats they face and how to prioritize among them. This type of broad-based sharing of widely used threat techniques can help neutralize unsophisticated actors and force sophisticated adversaries, such as nation-state actors, to develop new (and therefore costlier) techniques. This narrowing of the threat landscape can enable public and private organizations to more effectively target high-priority and advanced persistent adversaries and threats.

4. Incident response and recovery.—CTA cyber threat information sharing will lead to better information, particularly about adversary playbooks, that can make incident response and recovery efforts faster and more effective.

To fulfill these core missions, the CTA has built an automated cyber threat information-sharing platform with the goal of enabling and incentivizing the sharing of high-quality, actionable cyber threat information. The CTA and its platform embody a major step forward in transforming shared cyber threat information into effective preventive measures that can automatically be deployed by CTA members to their respective customers. The CTA platform is not just a concept or a set of Powerpoint slides—it is a functioning system, actively working to protect its members and their customers in near-real-time, and thus contributing to the increased protection of the industry and the world.

For example, recently, a single shared cyber threat sample from one CTA member allowed another member to build protections before that organization's customers were targeted—preventing successful attacks against 29 subsequent organizations. In another instance, cyber threat data shared through the CTA from one member allowed another member to identify a targeted attack against its customer and release additional indicators to defend that organization. The CTA and its platform have shown that a well-designed and well-built cyber threat information-sharing program can improve the Nation's cyber defenses and undermine the efforts of cyber adversaries. CTA is already improving cybersecurity, with some members finding that 40 to 50 percent of CTA's shared cyber threat data is new and directly actionable.

BETTER CYBERSECURITY

The cyber threats we face as a world are very serious. For over 40 years, the United States and other like-minded countries have used the internet and cyber space to derive enormous benefits: Economic growth, National security improvements, and social well-being. However, if we do not begin to effectively address the cyber threats we face, those benefits could wither. That is not a future we want. Tackling this challenge effectively will require forging new partnerships within industries, between industries, and between the Government and industry. It will require organizations to adopt new mindsets and change old beliefs to reflect the realities of the modern cyber threat environment. It will require coordinated action in a manner that reinforces market forces and competition. The Cyber Threat Alliance is ready to do its part in this endeavor and achieve effective cybersecurity for everyone around the world.

Chairman MCCAUL. Thank you, Mr. Daniel. You stayed right on time. I appreciate that.

Mr. Cilluffo.

STATEMENT OF FRANK J. CILLUFFO, DIRECTOR, CENTER FOR CYBER AND HOMELAND SECURITY, GEORGE WASHINGTON UNIVERSITY

Mr. CILLUFFO. Since I barely had an unspoken thought, I will try to be brief.

But, Mr. Chairman McCaul, Congressman Thompson, distinguished Members of the committee, thank you for the opportunity to appear before you today.

To piggyback on some of the comments that General Alexander and Michael Daniel brought up, we face a dizzying array of cyber threats coming at us from all directions. I mean, literally you blink and you have missed the latest hack de jour.

I think what we all can also recognize is that the threat tempo is accelerating and magnified by the speed at which technology evolves and the fact that we are expanding the attack surface through entities such as the Internet of Things; but also by the fact that our adversaries continue to adapt their tactics, techniques, and procedures, or their TTPs, to defeat our prevention and response measures. This is not a static set of issues, and we have got to look at it through both lenses and perspectives.

No one is immune—not our Government, not our businesses, and not any of us as individuals. But not all hacks are the same, nor are all hackers or their targets.

I think we face a signal-to-noise dilemma right now. Who and what do we need to pay attention to, and why?

I will try to be very brief on laying out some of the threat actors because I hope we will have some time to get through that during Q&A, but the threat comes in various shapes, sizes, and forms. At the high end we are dealing with nation-state actors, to criminal enterprises, to foreign terrorist organizations, to hacktivists, and script kiddies.

Just as diverse as the threat actors themselves is the wide variance in their intentions, capabilities, and the tools at their disposal. While I will pick on four particular countries, because they are the greatest threat emanating, from the—from a U.S. perspective, it is important to keep in mind that every country that has a modern military and intelligence service also has a computer network attack capability.

Nation-states also vary in their intentions, and some are more willing to exercise their cyber capabilities to disruptive and destructive attacks. Think North Korea; think Iran.

Indeed, the line between the ability to exploit and the ability to attack is paper-thin and turns simply upon the question of intent. If you can exploit you can also attack, if your intention is there to do so.

I think it is also important to recognize when we look at all these threat actors we can't look at cyber in isolation of the broader political and military components of these countries. So you can't just look at cyber. It is a tool in their toolkit to enable some of their overall primary objectives.

One thing that is compounding the challenge today is that countries are often turning to proxies to do their bidding. They do so for a whole host of reasons: To augment some of their capabilities that they may lack, or obviously to obscure the—to not send the muddy footprints back to their doorstep, to provide some plausible deniability. This is what I found most startling out of the Yahoo indictments, is just how explicit Russia's role was in terms of turning to cyber criminals to perpetrate these particular crimes.

Topping the list, from a threat perspective, no surprise to anyone here: Russia and China. Why? Because they are actually integrating computer network attack and exploit into their warfighting capability and doctrine. That is what differentiates them from other state actors.

The one note I would underscore from Monday's hearings before the House Permanent Select Committee on Intelligence was the banter between Director Comey and Admiral Rogers on whether or not this will facilitate and embolden Russia to continue to engage in these sorts of attacks. They were talking about 2018, 2020.

But in addition to Russia, what other countries are observing—what are they getting out of our mealy-mouth and weak response? I think that is a fair—all sides are to blame on that one. That is not a current situation.

But I think we need to get to the point where we can start articulating a cyber deterrent strategy.

Just two other points on Russia and China that I think are important: In addition to serving as threat actors, they also provide virtual safe havens for a number of these criminal enterprises, and we don't have extradition treaties. So law enforcement is really stymied in their ability to bring hackers to justice, and vast majority of these hackers are in Russia and China.

Very briefly, what Russia—when you are thinking about countries that are not only looking to computer network exploit and warfighting capabilities, obviously topping that list is North Korea and Iran. What they may lack in intent—in capability they make up for with intent, and they are turning to more and more destructive attacks.

Iran has got a long history in doing so, and I think we need to keep an especially close eye on North Korea, given their recalcitrant behavior right now and given the fact that, ironically, they are not only engaged in computer network attack, but they have turned to cyber crime to basically fund the regime since they have been entirely isolated by the international economy.

With that, I did go over. Sorry, Mr. Chairman. I hope to get to some of these questions during the Q&A.

[The prepared statement of Mr. Cilluffo follows:]

PREPARED STATEMENT OF FRANK J. CILLUFFO

MARCH 22, 2017

Chairman McCaul, Ranking Member Thompson, and distinguished committee Members thank you for the opportunity to testify before you today on this subject of National importance. As cyber threats continue to multiply and evolve, your resolve to explore this complex yet critical area is commendable. My testimony will focus primarily on the nature of the threat—including how to think about the major threat actors and their behavior—but will also contain thoughts on how best to respond to the vexing economic and National security challenges associated with America's digital footprint.

As individuals, businesses, and Government entities choose to increasingly utilize the advantages of the internet, they expand their exposure to the security vulnerabilities of information technologies that ever more sophisticated and persistent threat actors seek to leverage for political or monetary gain. Magnifying the security problems of growing vulnerabilities and already thinly stretched cybersecurity resources, the threat tempo is accelerating. This is due to a variety of factors including the continued advantage of offense over defense in cyber space, the added efficiencies associated with division of labor and specialization in the maturing economy for cyber crime, and the weak deterrent force of nascent policy responses that have yet to fully account for the diverse and transnational nature of cyber threats. The first step to addressing the policy problems created by these trends is to seek to understand the complexities of the cyber threat. In order to do so, we should conceive of it as a spectrum upon which the many and varied threat actors can be placed. Not all hacks and not all hackers are the same. To the contrary both intentions and capabilities vary widely:

Nation-states.—At the high end of the spectrum are nation-states whose military and intelligence services are both determined and sophisticated in the cyber domain. Russia, China, Iran, and North Korea presently top the list; but it is important to understand that every country with a modern military and intelligence service now possesses computer network exploitation (CNE) and computer network attack (CNA) capability. Indeed the line between the ability to exploit and the ability to attack is reed-thin and turns simply upon the question of intent. Also keep in mind that cyber strategy and tactics must be understood in context—as part and parcel of other geopolitical tools and goals (military, political, economic)—not in isolation from them.

Nation-states often use proxies to do their bidding. Countries do so for a range of reasons including to augment capabilities or to obfuscate the true source of the intrusion or attack thereby affording plausible deniability. Depending upon the reason(s) for which their services have been engaged, the proxy may be state-sponsored, state-supported or state-sanctioned.

In previous testimony before this committee I have discussed in detail the capabilities and intentions of the four leading threat actors.[1] Building on that baseline, today I will highlight the latest developments regarding these countries. Note however that the most sophisticated threats that we face emanate from Russia and China which have both integrated CNA and CNE into their warfighting strategy and doctrine.

Russia.—Russia has a long history of cyber aggression against other nations; to wit: Estonia (2007), Georgia (2008), and Ukraine (2014–15, and continuing). Russian efforts persisted in 2016–17, with attempts to interfere in the U.S. election, and information operations targeting multiple countries in both eastern and western Europe—including those with upcoming elections, such as France and Germany. Russia has been particularly adept at integrating cyber into its strategic plans and operations. In February 2017, Russia's Defense Minister acknowledged that the country had created a new military branch: "information warfare troops."[2]

In the cases of Ukraine and Georgia, Russia combined cyber and kinetic operations; and in the case of Ukraine, Russia is believed to have perpetrated the first-ever electricity blackout caused by computer network attack. In recent years, Russia has demonstrated an increasing level of assertiveness in the cyber domain, showing—in the words of then-Director of National Intelligence James Clapper—a "willingness to target critical infrastructure systems and conduct espionage operations even when detected."[3]

In 2009, the *Wall Street Journal* reported that cyber-spies from Russia (and China) had penetrated the U.S. electrical grid, leaving behind software programs, and trying to navigate the systems and their controls. What purpose could the mapping of U.S. critical infrastructure serve, other than intelligence preparation of the battlefield? The NASDAQ exchange too has allegedly been the target of a "complex hack" by a nation-state; again one questions the motivation.

In Russia, the forces of crime, business, and politics have long converged in a toxic blend; and there is evidence of complicity between the Russian government and cyber criminals and hackers. Over time, Russian hackers believed to be doing their government's bidding have breached the White House, the State Department, and the Defense Department.

China.—China has demonstrated a remarkable level of persistence evidenced by the sheer number of acts of espionage that the country has committed. These aggressive collection efforts have amassed secrets (military—including plans for the F–35, commercial/proprietary, etc.) in order to propel China's economic growth, military power, and technological & scientific capacities—and thereby gain strategic advantage in relation to (actual and perceived) competitor countries and adversaries.

---

[1] See for example: Statement of Frank J. Cilluffo before the U.S. House of Representatives, Committee on Homeland Security, Subcommittee on Cybersecurity, Infrastructure Protection and Security Technologies, "Emerging Cyber Threats to the United States," February 25, 2016. *https://cchs.gwu.edu/sites/cchs.gwu.edu/files/downloads/HHSC_Testimony_Feb%2025-2016_Final.pdf.* Also see the resource document, Samantha F. Ravich and Annie Fixler, "Framework and Terminology for Understanding Cyber-Enabled Economic Warfare," Foundation for Defense of Democracies, February 22, 2017. *http://www.defenddemocracy.org/content/uploads/documents/22217_Cyber_Definitions.pdf.*

[2] Vladimir Isachenkov, "Russia Military Acknowledges New Branch: Info Warfare Troops," The Associated Press, February 22, 2017. *http://www.bigstory.ap.org/article/8b7532462dd0495d9f756c9ae7d2ff3c/russian-military-continues-massive-upgrade.*

[3] James R. Clapper, Director of National Intelligence, "Worldwide Threat Assessment of the U.S. Intelligence Community," Statement for the Record before the U.S. Senate, Armed Services Committee, February 9, 2016. *http://www.dni.gov/files/documents/SASC_Unclassified_2016_ATA_SFR_FINAL.pdf.*

In May 2015, data theft on a massive scale, affecting virtually all U.S. Government employees, was traced back to China. The extent to which the information gleaned from this hack of the U.S. Office of Personnel Management (OPM) may be used to blackmail and recruit Americans, to China's benefit, remains to be seen.

In September 2015, China and the United States reached an agreement on refraining from conducting economic cyber espionage. Initially this agreement appeared to reduce the level of activity, although it may simply have pushed China's efforts in a different direction: Greater efforts directed at U.S. Government (rather than U.S. corporate) targets can be expected, moving forward; in addition, a notable spike in Chinese cyber activity in the region (China's "neighborhood") has been observed. Since the 2015 Obama-Xi agreement, moreover, China appears to have shifted from use of the People's Liberation Army (PLA) to relying more on its security and intelligence services for a greater role in hacking foreign companies. However military officers in China are increasingly known to moonlight as hackers for hire, when off the clock. While Russia has received an overwhelming amount of attention during the past year, this should not detract from the cyber activities and threat posed by other state actors.

Iran.—Iran has invested heavily in recent years in order to deepen and expand its cyber warfare capabilities, although this capacity was initially directed internally to repress democratic forces in the country. This effort came in the wake of the Stuxnet worm, which targeted Iran's nuclear weapons development program. In recent years Iran has engaged in a concerted cyber campaign against U.S. banks. U.S. officials also believe Iran to be responsible for a cyber attack against the Sands Casino in Las Vegas owned by politically active billionaire Sheldon Adelson; the attack wiped clean many hard drives and sought to destroy corporate infrastructure. Hackers linked to the Iranian government have also used cyber means to compromise the control system of a dam north of New York City. Iran has long relied heavily on proxies such as Hezbollah—which now has a companion organization, Cyber Hezbollah—to strike at perceived adversaries. Iran and Hezbollah are believed to have perpetrated the cyber attacks against Saudi Aramco and Qatari RasGas, which compromised 30,000 computers. Elements of Iran's Revolutionary Guard Corps (IRGC) have also relied upon proxy forces including political/criminal hackers, to work on behalf of the regime.

Iran is expected to hold a Presidential election in May 2017. Should a hard-line candidate prevail, there may well be a further uptick in the country's aggressive behavior in cyber space. U.S.-Iran relations moving forward are yet to be fully defined, given that there is also a new administration in the United States that has been in office for just 2 months. However the Joint Comprehensive Program of Action (JCPOA) regarding Iran's nuclear program looms large in the background. Depending upon U.S. actions and policy in this area—including whether the administration retains the agreement and how it handles the matter of sanctions against Iran—the Iranian regime may decide to act out further in the cyber domain. Notably the JCPOA has resulted in substantial funds being placed in Iranian hands through sanctions relief. The regime will likely devote these funds to the further expansion of its cyber capabilities (offensive/defensive) and should either party move to annul the agreement, we can expect a significant increase in cyber activity against U.S. interests and assets.

North Korea.—Many of the details about North Korea's cyber warfare capabilities are shrouded in secrecy (the same is true of their military capabilities writ large). What we do know is that, much like Iran, North Korea has invested heavily in building cyber capabilities. A recent report by the South Korean Defense Ministry estimates that the North Korean "cyber army" employs an elite squad of 6,000 hackers, many of whom operate abroad in northeast China and throughout South East Asia.[4] And what North Korea lacks in capability it makes up for with intent (again, like Iran). North Korea has shown little restraint, engaging in computer network attack—disruptive and/or destructive attacks (rather than espionage).

In recent months, there has been a major increase in North Korean cyber attacks (attempted and successful) targeting South Korean companies and government.[5] Senior Japanese cybersecurity officials confirmed this in recent meetings, and expressed significant concern about both the increase in volume and aggressiveness of North Korean cyber activity. Outside the region, North Korea also operates with-

---

[4] Martin Anderson, "North Korea's Internet Tundra Breeds Specialised "Cyber Forces" Numbering 6,000," The Stack, January 7, 2015. *https://thestack.com/security/2015/01/07/north-koreas-internet-tundra-breeds-specialised-cyber-forces-numbering-6000/*.

[5] Charlie Campbell, "The World Can Expect More Cybercrime from North Korea Now that China has Banned its Coal," Time, February 19, 2017. *http://time.com/4676204/north-korea-cyber-crime-hacking-china-coal/*.

out compunction, targeting U.S. companies; The most notorious case is their attack on Sony Pictures Entertainment. Recent news articles revealing alleged U.S. cyber activities aimed at stymieing North Korea's ballistic missile program will likely serve to increase the likelihood of additional North Korean cyber attacks.

North Korea has long turned to illicit activity such as counterfeiting (of bills, pharmaceuticals, and cigarettes) to fill its coffers. More recently the country has turned to cyber crime and is the prime suspect in a string of bank heists. The latest round of U.N. economic sanctions aimed at North Korea, coupled with China's suspension of coal imports to the country, suggest we ought to be prepared for a spike in North Korean state-sponsored and/or state-supported cyber crime.

Criminal Enterprises.—After nation-states, criminal organizations are the next most capable threat actors. Increasingly, the capabilities that used to be the exclusive preserve of nation-states are now in the hands of criminal entities [6]—which outstrip the present abilities of foreign terrorist organizations (FTOs) in this particular regard. Criminal groups are motivated by profit rather than politics or ideology, yet their pursuit of monetary gain often has broader impacts on the integrity of the global economic system which in turn is closely linked to international security. Cyber space allows criminals to take their malicious activities to a global scale. Powerful organizations, like the recently dismantled Avalanche criminal network can thus create cyber crime tools and infrastructure that can bring malicious actors together so that they may collectively pose a transnational threat to the operations of governments and private entities.[7] The cross-border and interjurisdictional approach of Europol and its partners in the United States and elsewhere to take down the Avalanche group is a testament to the resources and coordination required to effectively address such threats.[8] It is important to note that while cyber criminals are unlikely to ever have the ability to collect and use all-source intelligence as governments can, the gap between the capabilities of sophisticated cyber criminals and nation-states is increasingly narrowing. Compounding this challenge is that fact that criminal groups are working ever-more either with or for nation-states such as Russia. The Yahoo hack (2014) that compromised 500 million user-accounts and led to the recent indictment of four individuals—two FSB (Russian domestic intelligence) officers and two cyber criminals—is a case that demonstrates the willingness of states to utilize criminals for hire as proxies.[9]

This convergence of nation-state and criminal forces heightens the dangers posed by both; and also makes it difficult to discern just who is master and who is puppet. Traditionally it has been the forces of crime that seek to penetrate the state; yet in the case of North Korea for example, the opposite is true: The regime engages criminal proxies and their cyber prowess to help achieve the ends that will perpetuate the regime's survival. This tactic is easier than ever to pursue with the emergence of the market model of "Crime-as-a-Service,"[10] which facilitates cyber crime by making the tools and skills needed for it more readily accessible to a wider variety of actors. Compounding the challenge for law enforcement, nations such as Russia and China amount to virtual safe havens for cyber criminals since the United States lacks extradition treaties with these countries.

Foreign Terrorist Organizations.—For Foreign Terrorist Organizations (FTOs) there is no shortage of motivation or intent but fortunately, FTOs have yet to fully develop a sustained cyber-attack capability. While this is reassuring to a certain extent, it does not mean that such actors pose no threat in the cyber domain. Even outside of the cyber context, the most pressing threats from terrorist organizations stem from their ability to execute asymmetric, "no-warning" attacks, that do not rise to the level of impact associated with persistent state-to-state competition or conflict. Nevertheless, such operations can endanger the lives of civilians and interfere with the integrity of critical infrastructure. Therefore, while FTOs are not likely to

---

[6] Doug Olenick, "Cybercriminal's skills now on par with nation states: Mandiant," SC Magazine, March 14, 2017. *https://www.scmagazine.com/cybercriminals-skills-now-on-par-with-nation-states-mandiant/article/644124/.*

[7] Brian Krebs, "Avalanche Global Fraud Ring Dismantled," Krebs on Security, December 16, 2016. *https://krebsonsecurity.com/2016/12/avalanche-global-fraud-ring-dismantled/.*

[8] "Avalanche Network Dismantled in International Cyber Operation," Europol, December 1, 2016. *https://www.europol.europa.eu/newsroom/news/%E2%80%98avalanche%E2%80%99-network-dismantled-in-international-cyber-operation.*

[9] Department of Justice, "U.S. Charges Russian FSB Officers and Their Criminal Conspirators for Hacking Yahoo and Millions of Email Accounts," March 15, 2017. *https://www.justice.gov/opa/pr/us-charges-russian-fsb-officers-and-their-criminal-conspirators-hacking-yahoo-and-millions.*

[10] EUROPOL, European Union, Serious and Organised Crime Threat Assessment, 2017: Crime in the age of technology. *https://www.europol.europa.eu/activities-services/main-reports/european-union-serious-and-organised-crime-threat-assessment-2017.*

pose a catastrophic risk to the homeland or America's economy in the near future, it would be imprudent to ignore the efforts of these actors to utilize the internet to their advantage and acquire cyber capabilities that they can then integrate with kinetic force to execute the equivalent of a cyber drive-by shooting.

Those FTOs that are currently most concerning from a cyber threat standpoint are entities that benefit from state support or sponsorship and those affiliated with the Islamic State in Iraq and Syria. The Western world has already seen the troublesome effects of ISIS' use of the internet to spread propaganda and radicalize vulnerable populations, but their efforts do not stop there. Members of ISIS have repeatedly utilized a tactic known as "doxing" to target U.S. military and law enforcement personnel through the strategic release of their stolen personal information and social media intelligence collection. Also of note, a group known as the United Cyber Caliphate (UCC), which increasingly appears to be functioning as a cyber arm of ISIS, has touted its accomplishments in the realms of hacking and DDoS attacks, and has announced plans to launch a cyber attack against the United States in the near future. America's efforts to target high-value leaders of ISIS, including its most prolific cyber aggressors Junaid Hussain and the UCC's Osed Agha, have demonstrated their capacity to successfully set back ISIS' cyber capabilities. Such groups deserve the continued attention of security officials, especially in cases where they can leverage associations with other malicious actors to augment their cyber capabilities.

Hacktivists.—Whether acting alone or loosely in tandem, hacktivists may possess considerable skill and cause significant disruption when they perceive their core interests to be at stake. Oftentimes, hacking collectives such as Anonymous, can leverage their sheer numbers to overwhelm servers and shut down websites or exploit vulnerabilities to bring attention to their cause of the day. While these movements lack the type of centralized command-and-control infrastructures that would make their influence more troubling, their sometimes populist appeal and dispersed manpower allow them to operate in unique ways that undermine American security interests.

While hacktivists, including malicious insiders, vary in degree of sophistication and tend to be leaderless, their ability to spread discord on-line can augment existing digital vulnerabilities and reinforce the efforts of other malicious cyber actors. Therefore, they should not be discounted when assessing the wider cyber threat spectrum. Even in the case of unsophisticated hacktivists, who may not possess extensive "in-house" cyber expertise, we must consider the increasing ease with which such malicious actors can simply buy or rent the requisite tools or services on the Deep Web and Darknet(s). Only a small percentage of the material available on the internet is indexed and accessible from standard search engines. Beneath the surface web that we all see is the unindexed Deep Web and its subcomponent, the Darknet, which can only be accessed through password protected sites or when using specific software such as TOR or I2P.[11] It is in such realms of the internet that malicious actors—including FTOs—buy and sell hacking tools and expertise and fence stolen information. As the ability to trade in malicious cyber expertise becomes more prevalent, it is in fact necessary to consider the impacts of this trend in all threat assessments, agnostic to the specific actor in question.

CYBER DOMAIN: CHARACTERISTICS, EVOLUTION, AND VULNERABILITIES

In the cyber domain, the advantage lies with the attacker. At the same time, the surface of attack has expanded exponentially with the advent of the Internet of Things. However, the dynamism of this environment should not be underestimated and we must recognize that the capabilities of both attackers and defenders in cyber space are continually changing. Looking ahead, U.S. officials warn that simple theft or disruption of data may give way to data manipulation.[12]

Increasingly, threat actors are setting their sights on America's critical infrastructure which cuts across the public and private sectors. While the United States approach of designating 16 sectors critical is sound, not all of these sectors are equally critical. What are known as the "lifeline" sectors—in particular, the energy and electric sectors, water, telecommunications, transportation, and financial services—have an even greater impact on public safety and security than the others.

The potential for cascading effects if any of these were rendered inoperative or dysfunctional, especially for a significant length of time, further magnifies their im-

---

[11] "Illuminating the Deep and Dark Web: The Next Frontier in Comprehensive IT Security," Flashpoint Intel, 2015. *https://www.flashpoint-intel.com/book/illuminating-deep-dark-web.*

[12] Spencer Ackerman, "Newest cyber threat will be data manipulation, US intelligence chief says," The Guardian, September 10, 2015. *https://www.theguardian.com/technology/2015/sep/10/cyber-threat-data-manipulation-us-intelligence-chief.*

portance. From the standpoint of prevention and response, it is these areas that should be treated as top priority (while bearing in mind the adage that if everything is a priority then nothing truly is). Section 9 of Executive Order 13636 on Improving Critical Infrastructure Cybersecurity provides the framework for a "risk-based approach" of this type.[13]

Examples of cyber incidents and intrusions are regrettably plentiful, but a few cases merit mention here in order to bring into sharper relief some of the concepts referenced above:

SWIFT Hacks.—The first case that rises above the noise and warrants attention is the theft of $81 million from the Central Bank of Bangladesh in February 2016 and similar yet less successful attempts at other major banks in the developing world. In the case of Bangladesh Bank, it would have been a $950 million heist had the request not set off alarms due to a coincidental similarity between the address of a bank in which hackers sought to deposit their stolen funds and the name of a corporation sanctioned by the U.S. Government.[14] Although $81 million is a significant sum, the loss of which doubtlessly had significant, negative impacts on the bank and its clients, the global economy can absorb relatively minor losses such as this one. From the perspective of security officials, the real worry is how hackers perpetrated this crime and the systemic vulnerabilities in the global financial order that such a cyber heist publicly highlighted. The hackers stole the credentials of target banks to gain access to SWIFT, the interbank messaging system that connects 11,000 banks and financial institutions globally and settles billions of dollars of transactions daily. From there, hackers were able to place illegitimate requests for transfers of funds that most banks fulfill automatically.[15]

These attacks exposed a potential single-point-of-failure in a system that modern economies depend upon every day. We still do not know the full extent to which hackers have compromised SWIFT's member-banks, but SWIFT recently disclosed that its members have suffered a number of other hacking incidents through its messaging infrastructure in the last year, in which about one in five resulted in stolen funds.[16]

The Carbanak Gang.—In 2013, the so-called Carbanak gang perpetrated a series of well-orchestrated assaults on eastern European and Russian banks. Named after the malware used, the Carbanak gang compromised internal bank systems and sent commands directly to ATMs (a scheme known as "ATM jackpotting") throughout eastern Europe, causing the machines to dispense cash. More than 100 banks spanning 11 countries were hit—with losses of hundreds of millions of dollars—highlighting just how much damage cyber-criminals can do.[17] The activities of the Carbanak gang continue unabated with new techniques at their disposal and new targets in their crosshairs.

Energy Grid Attacks.—On December 24, 2015, western Ukraine experienced a power outage that is believed to have been caused by cyber attack perpetrated by Russia. Though just one power company reported the incident, "similar malware was found in the networks of at least two other utilities."[18] More than 4 dozen substations were affected, as were more than a quarter of a million customers for up to 6 hours. In addition, a simultaneous attack on call centers (a telephony denial-of-service attack) hindered communication and customer reporting of difficulties. The case is truly significant: It is believed to represent the first time that a blackout was caused by computer network attack. But it would not be the last: Again, in December 2016, Ukraine witnessed a cyber attack on their power grid, leaving part of Kiev without power. Once more, all the evidence points to Russia (or its proxies) as perpetrator. These incidents represent a crossing of the Rubicon: A cyber attack

---

[13] February 12, 2013. *https://www.gpo.gov/fdsys/pkg/FR-2013-02-19/pdf/2013-03915.pdf.*

[14] Krishna Das and Jonathan Spicer, "How the New York Fed Fumbled of the Bangladesh Bank Cyber-Heist," Reuters, July 21, 2016. *http://www.reuters.com/investigates/special-report/cyber-heist-Federal/.*

[15] Devlin Barrett and Katy Burne, "Now It's Three: Ecuador Bank Hacked via Swift," The Wall Street Journal, May 19, 2016. *https://www.wsj.com/articles/lawsuit-claims-another-global-banking-hack-1463695820.*

[16]. Tom Bergen and Jim Finkle, "Exclusive: SWIFT Confirms New Cyber Thefts, Hacking Tactics," Reuters, December 12, 2016. *http://www.reuters.com/article/us-usa-cyber-swift-exclusive-idUSKBN1412NT.*

[17] David E. Sanger and Nicole Perlroth, "Bank Hackers Steal Millions via Malware," The New York Times, February 14, 2015. *https://www.nytimes.com/2015/02/15/world/bank-hackers-steal-millions-via-malware.html?partner=socialflow&smid=tw-nytimes&_r=2;* Brian Krebs, "Carbanak Gang Tied to Russian Security Firm?" Krebs on Security, July 18, 2016. *https://krebsonsecurity.com/2016/07/carbanak-gang-tied-to-russian-security-firm/.*

[18] Reuters, "Experts: Ukraine Utility Cyberattack Wider than Reported," Voice of America, January 5, 2016. *http://www.voanews.com/a/reu-experts-ukraine-utility-cyberattack-wider-than-reported/3131554.html.*

creating real-world, physical implications. The attacks thus sent a message that was loud and clear.

Mirai Botnet.—Botnets, or networks of internet-connected devices that unbeknownst to their legitimate users can be centrally controlled to perpetrate malicious cyber activities on a grand scale, have been around for a long time. However, this past fall, the Mirai botnet demonstrated how the concept of distributed computing power and centralized command-and-control can leverage the rampant insecurity associated with the expanding Internet of Things environment. Malicious actors used the botnet, which was primarily made up of vulnerable webcams and internet routers, to execute the most powerful DDoS attack in history against the computer security blogger Brian Krebs.[19] More alarmingly, the Mirai botnet later used a DDoS attack to target Dyn, which supports much of the internet's infrastructure, and successfully interrupted the services of Spotify, Twitter, and PayPal for millions of users.[20] The cases of the Mirai botnet's DDoS attacks are significant because they are just the beginning of what security officials can expect from malicious actors seeking to leverage the digital vulnerabilities of IoT devices and the wide-spread ignorance or apathy of IoT producers and consumers to these security concerns. Society must begin to consider security over convenience and necessity over luxury when connecting devices, even those that seem relatively innocuous, to the internet. Otherwise, malicious actors will continue to benefit from the bountiful harvest of vulnerable devices ready to be recruited for criminal and other malicious purposes. Currently, estimates show that around tens of billions of devices will be connected to the internet by 2020, an exponential growth in connectivity that runs parallel to a growth in the digital attack surface.[21]

U.S. RESPONSE

The many and varied cyber threats that the United States faces requires a multidimensional response. While the United States should continue to invest in its offensive cyber capabilities to, as best as possible, ensure its superiority and escalatory dominance, a powerful defensive component is essential to America's cybersecurity and underlies all the rest. Resources and funding should therefore be balanced between offensive and defensive capacity building. A clearly articulated deterrence strategy is also needed, but remains in its infancy—although the recent Defense Science Board report on the subject is a solid step in the right direction.[22] An effective cyber deterrence strategy should utilize various levers of state power to affect the cost-benefit analysis of malicious actors by denying them benefits by demonstrating America's capability and willingness to impose costs on such malicious actors. Cyber deterrence requires more than military underpinnings and the same is true of U.S. cyber response more generally. Public-private partnerships are instrumental to cybersecurity; and the public sector component of that equation includes not only Federal entities but also their State and local counterparts. Whether partnering with companies or State and Local officials, the Department of Homeland Security (DHS) plays an important and meaningful role in terms of enabling U.S. responses to cyber threats, distinct from the Department of Defense mandate in this area.

Cybersecurity requires both a whole-of-Government and whole-of-society approach. Government alone cannot get us to where we need to be. Industry and even individuals must each do their part; and industry sectors must collaborate within bounds (with competitor companies) as well as across bounds (with other sectors and with government at all levels). Developments such as the expansion of the Internet of Things serve to reinforce these imperatives.

Private-sector initiatives of the type needed are already under way. The financial services sector in particular is leading the way with its Information Sharing and Analysis Center (FS–ISAC), a global industry forum for cyber (and physical) threat intelligence analysis and sharing; and with the Financial Systemic Analysis and Resilience Center (FSARC), intended to deepen threat analysis and mitigate systemic

---

[19] Lily Hay Newman, "The Botnet that Broke the Internet Isn't Going Away," Wired, December 9, 2016. *https://www.wired.com/2016/12/botnet-broke-internet-isnt-going-away/*.

[20] Brian Krebs, "Did the Mirai Botnet Really take Liberia Offline?" Krebs on Security, November 4, 2016. *https://krebsonsecurity.com/tag/mirai-botnet/*.

[21] BI Intelligence, "Here's How the Internet of Things Will Explode by 2020," Business Insider, August 31 2016. *http://www.businessinsider.com/iot-ecosystem-internet-of-things-forecasts-and-business-opportunities-2016-2*.

[22] Department of Defense, Task Force on Cyber Deterrence, February 2017. *http://www.acq.osd.mil/dsb/reports/2010's/DSB-CyberDeterrenceReport_02-28-17_Final.pdf*.

risk.[23] To lead and respond effectively however, companies require the tools to do so—which is why the FSARC works together with Government partners including DHS, whose expertise complements that of industry members.

More broadly, the private sector as a whole must be empowered to respond proactively and robustly in the face of cyber threats. Businesses never expected to find themselves on the front lines of cyber battle, facing sophisticated adversaries with nation-state capabilities. In such circumstances, companies must take steps (ahead of time or in real-time) to protect their data and networks, particularly their crown jewels. In turn, Government has a responsibility to clarify the parameters of acceptable corporate action so that businesses fully understand what they can and cannot do in this regard. For those areas deemed outside corporate jurisdiction, Government has a responsibility to step in and support/protect the targeted entities and assets. Regrettably the discussion surrounding these issues has been less than nuanced to date; yet there is much that can be done in terms of active defense, apart from the two poles of doing nothing at all or "hacking back."[24] Public and private sector actors should work to jointly develop the private sector's capacity and authorities to utilize active defenses, capabilities that when developed and marshalled responsibly, can begin to flip the equation and give cyber defenders a fighting chance.

The operating principles set out above (e.g., the need for a whole-of-Government approach and public-private partnerships) is equally important at the international level. Alliances between the U.S. Department of Defense and other nation-states' military services—such as NATO—are one crucial component of a solid response posture vis-à-vis cyber domain; but so too are non-military alliances between the United States and foreign governments and companies. While the Five Eyes alliance has served us well over time and will continue to play an integral role in our National security, it may be that a new and broader grouping is needed in order to tackle cyber threats more effectively. A transnational threat requires a transnational solution and it may be constructive to bring together like-minded states with substantial cyber assets in a new international forum with a mandate of responding to international cyber threats.

Returning to DHS, from the standpoint of structure and legislation—and in particular how best to organize the bureaucracy for cybersecurity and infrastructure protection purposes—what matters most at the end of the day is the effective execution of the mission. It is important to emphasize that while the Department of Defense's role in defending the Nation against foreign cyber threats is significant, supporting its initiatives should not come at the cost of neglecting the equally important role that DHS plays in protecting critical infrastructure and civilian government networks. In this context, there have been a number of efforts to legislatively address issues related to DHS resourcing and organization. As this committee works to continue these efforts—including progress on its own legislation, the following principles (which are largely consistent with the committee's proposed legislation) should be taken into account: The relevant entities and officials within DHS must possess the necessary authorities and resources to fulfill their cybersecurity missions; and they must be held accountable for their actions through clear lines of responsibility and the application of metrics and measurable goals. Furthermore, as challenges related to the recruitment and retention of necessary cyber talent persist, DHS should also be able to utilize streamlined and flexible hiring authorities to fill cyber positions with qualified individuals in a timely manner. These principles matter more than the wiring diagram per se, if we can agree that implementation is paramount.

Thank you again for the opportunity to testify on such a crucial challenge to America's economic and National security. I look forward to answering any questions you may have.

Chairman MCCAUL. Thanks, Frank.
Chair recognizes Mr. McConnell.

---

[23] Michael Chertoff and Frank Cilluffo, "Trump Administration Can Help Finance Sector Shift Cybersecurity Paradigm," Forbes, January 18, 2017. *https://www.forbes.com/sites/realspin/2017/01/18/trump-administration-can-help-finance-sector-shift-cybersecurity-paradigm/#72d07-df0645d.*

[24] For details, see "Into the Gray Zone: The Private Sector and Active Defense Against Cyber Threats," CCHS Project Report, October 2016. *https://cchs.gwu.edu/sites/cchs.gwu.edu/files/downloads/CCHS-ActiveDefenseReportFINAL.pdf.*

STATEMENT OF BRUCE W. MC CONNELL, GLOBAL VICE PRESIDENT, EASTWEST INSTITUTE

Mr. McConnell. Morning, Chairman McCaul, Ranking Member Thompson, and distinguished Members of the committee. Thank you for inviting me.

I am Bruce McConnell, from the EastWest Institute, an independent, nonpartisan nonprofit that works with all major governments and the private sector to reduce security conflicts. Before EastWest I served 4 years at DHS, departing in 2013, as the acting deputy under secretary of cybersecurity. I also served at the OMB under Presidents Reagan, George H.W. Bush, and Clinton.

Let me tell you what keeps me awake at night, what got me out of bed this morning to come see you. Last week I hosted a meeting near my home in Oakland, California. Two hundred government officials, industry geeks, professors, and activists from 35 countries spent 3 days developing answers to Apple versus FBI, how to make smart cities into safe cities, improving capacity in cyber insurance, and, most important, developing rules of behavior for governments and companies in cyber space.

Have you ever seen your children or grandchildren swipe away the 25 smartphone apps they have open? Each of these apps enliven some aspect of their lives—of our lives. We are grateful for this technology, and it makes—we are dependent on it.

What is worrisome is that every one of those apps is an open door to well-funded, persistent, state-sponsored attackers to intrude on our business or deny us the benefits of cyber space. When I think about this for myself it makes me mad. However, when I multiply that by the 2 billion people and millions of companies that are on the network today, I foresee a—and the billions of young people who are coming on the years—in the years ahead—I foresee a global economic and political catastrophe unless we get those attackers under control.

Today's situation reminds me of the Gold Rush out in California 160 years ago. Some people made a lot of money and it developed one of the great States of our union. It also took us 30 years to establish law and order out there.

Mr. Chairman, we don't have 30 years to establish law and order in cyber space. Military and intelligence agencies all over the world are equipped with the latest computers, communications, and cyber weaponry. These are good weapons. They are cost-effective, they are generally non-lethal, and they let us project force remotely and often stealthily.

But there are two problems.

First, there is a runaway cyber arms race led by the United States, Russia, China, Iran, Israel, some European countries, and North Korea. Over 30 countries have formed cyber offense units. There is no deterrence, no incentive not to do so.

There is also an information war going on between East and West. It involves the cyber burglary and publication of stolen information, like during the U.S. elections. This is part of a larger, damaging degradation of the information space by the dissemination of fake news, political trolling, social media bots, and the weaponization of intelligence.

We know that the Russians and their surrogates are not the only attackers. There is always China, and earlier this month we learned about Western actions taken against North Korean missile systems and a variety of CIA practices.

Even with the best motivations, these continuing, ungoverned state-on-state skirmishes in cyber space undermine terrestrial security and stability. There is a growing risk of miscalculation and escalation that could spill over into direct physical harm to the United States and its citizens.

If the credibility of cyber space is further degraded it will be useless as a medium for commerce and governance. People are already leaving e-commerce because they are afraid they will be victimized.

So what should the U.S. Government do to respond? Fortunately, we have the answer to that question. In brief, we need cyber deterrence governed by rules, and we need cyber defense governed by roles.

Over the past two administrations the Executive branch worked on a bipartisan basis with this committee and with the rest of Congress to establish clear roles for cyber space security. The resulting laws and directives cemented the primary role of the Department of Homeland Security in protecting the Nation's critical cyber infrastructure, and in doing so they reflected two important values.

First, cyber space is fundamentally a civilian space. The military and the NSA in particular must protect our most valuable military and intelligence assets, but the military must keep out of our civilian infrastructure. It is a long National tradition, and they have their hands full already.

Second, securing cyber space is a team effort. Agencies must work with each other and with the private sector in a seamless manner.

In sum, the Government needs to buckle down, work with the private sector and with other governments, and get it done. It would be really great if you, on behalf of our kids and all the kids, could hold the Federal agencies accountable for what you have already told them to do.

Thank you, and I look forward to your questions.

[The prepared statement of Mr. McConnell follows:]

PREPARED STATEMENT OF BRUCE W. MCCONNELL

MARCH 22, 2017

I am Bruce W. McConnell, global vice president of the EastWest Institute, a 36-year-old, independent, non-partisan, non-profit organization dedicated to preventing and reducing security conflicts among nations on the ground and in cyber space. EWI works closely with senior Government and private-sector officials in all the major powers around the world to establish and support trustworthy dialog about some of the most difficult security issues facing the planet.

Before joining EWI I served for 4 years at the U.S. Department of Homeland Security (DHS), departing in 2013 as the acting deputy under secretary for cybersecurity. I also served at the U.S. Office of Management and Budget under Presidents Ronald Reagan, George H.W. Bush, and William Clinton, with responsibility for information technology policy and security.

This statement covers two topics: An assessment of the current state of conflict in cyber space, and my views on how the U.S. Government should address those conflicts.

HOW UNSTABLE IS CYBER SPACE TODAY?

Nearly 4 years ago U.S. national security advisor Susan Rice observed that the world's "most vexing security challenges are transnational security threats that transcend borders: Climate change, piracy, infectious disease, transnational crime, cyber theft, and the modern-day slavery of human trafficking." Today, one would add migration, violent extremism, and the safety of fissile nuclear materials to that list.

These issues share at least two characteristics: First they are accentuated in their severity by modern technology. The bad guys, both state and non-state actors, are well-equipped with the latest computers, communications equipment, and weaponry, and their ability to use these tools is enhanced by their access to global networks.

Second, no international regimes or institutions have these transborder issues well in hand. Rather, global bodies like the World Health Organization or the International Telecommunication Union are generally struggling to remain relevant. The post-war structures that have kept peace for 70 years face a crisis of legitimacy as rising powers that were not present at Bretton Woods scorn the old order and create their own institutions and power centers.

Today we are focusing on security and cyber space. Cyber-enabled attacks in the lead-up to the U.S. Presidential election roiled relationships in Washington and globally. The term cyber-enabled emphasizes a new characteristic of cyber space—it's no longer its own thing. It's part of everything. There is very little actual "cyber crime." Instead, we see a plethora of ordinary crimes and attacks: Theft, fraud, trespassing, and destruction of property that use cyber means.

From a geopolitical standpoint, this cyber-enablement has produced a runaway cyber arms race, led by the United States, Russia, China, Iran, Israel, and some European countries, with many others, including the Democratic People's Republic of Korea (DPRK), following close behind. Over 30 countries have formed cyber offense units. Non-state actors such as organized criminal gangs and the Islamic state are also players.

The U.S. Democratic National Committee hacks and related incidents consist of burglary and publication of the fruits on Wikileaks. From a legal standpoint, while it is against U.S. law to enter a computer without authorization, these incidents may fall more into the shadow zone of espionage. As for the publication, the U.S. Supreme Court has generally protected media publication of accurate, stolen materials of public interest obtained by a third party.

What's new for Americans is the possibility that there is an "information war" between East and West. Indeed, some states do not use the term cybersecurity, preferring the broader term "information security." The events around the U.S. election evoked a spirited conversation last month at the Munich Security Conference around fake news, political trolling, social media bots, and the weaponization of intelligence.[1]

On the other hand, earlier this month, we also saw additional evidence regarding Western actions against North Korean missile systems and the CIA's capabilities. Even assuming the most benign motivations by all parties, these continuing, ungoverned state-on-state skirmishes in cyber space increasingly undermine terrestrial security and stability.

In contrast to cyber space, other international domains are governed by norms of behavior and international law. In the airspace it is illegal to shoot down a commercial aircraft. But in cyber space, the way in which international law applies is still being debated.

In commercial aviation we have organizations like the private sector International Air Transport Association and the governmental International Commercial Aviation Organization that partner to maintain safety and security on a global basis. There are no comparable institutions for cyber space.

Everyone in this room is painfully familiar with the provisions that keep that network secure: Identity proofing of everyone who gets close to a passenger plane, licensing of pilots, filing of flight plans, certification of aircraft, etc. We have none of these things in cyber space. Yet the financial value of the commercial transactions conducted over the internet (and here I'm not even counting SWIFT and other special purpose networks) is actually 100 times greater on an annual basis than the value of goods transported in the air cargo system.

---

[1] U.S. Homeland Security Secretary John Kelly was on hand in Munich to remind European participants that DHS had reaffirmed the previous administration's designation of election systems as critical infrastructure and that the Department continued its work with state election officials to help them secure their systems on a voluntary basis.

Progress is modest. A group of governmental cyber experts has worked at the United Nations for over 10 years to come up with an initial set of non-binding norms of behavior in cyber space.

These include:

- Not allowing the use of information and communications technology, or ICT, to intentionally damage another country's critical infrastructure.
- Not allowing international cyber attacks to emanate from their territory.
- Responding to requests for assistance from another country that has been attacked by computers in the first country.
- Preventing the proliferation of malicious tools and techniques and the use of harmful hidden functions.
- Encouraging responsible reporting of ICT vulnerabilities and sharing associated information.
- Not harming the information systems of the authorized cybersecurity incident response teams.

In February 2017, the government of the Netherlands, with the support of Microsoft, the Internet Society, the EastWest Institute, and the Hague Centre for Strategic Studies, launched the Global Commission on the Stability of Cyberspace. The GCSC is chaired by Marina Kaljurand, former Estonian foreign minister, and co-chaired by Michael Chertoff, former U.S. Secretary of Homeland Security and Latha Reddy, India's former deputy National security adviser. This multi-stakeholder commission will build on and extend existing efforts to develop and advocate for norms and polices to enhance international security and stability and guide responsible state and non-state behavior in cyber space.

On the private-sector side, global ICT companies are beginning to step up to the responsibility that comes with their great power in cyber space. For example, Microsoft recently issued a set of norms of industry behavior that global ICT companies should follow in their business practices.

Examples of the kinds of norms that companies are considering include:

- Creating more secure products and services.
- Not enabling states to weaken the security of commercial, mass-market ICT products and services.
- Practicing responsible vulnerability disclosure.
- Collaborating to defend their customers against and recover from serious cyber attacks.
- Issuing updates to protect their customers no matter where the customer is located.

Clearly, the industry is at an immature stage. Its rapid growth in importance has outstripped systems of governance, including the first line of defense—the market. As a general matter, until very recently customers demanded two things from the firms that supply ICTs—price and features. The market has responded, giving us all manner of convenience and efficiency, in business and in our private lives. Finally, however, buyers are starting to recognize the criticality of ICT to their daily activities, and thus they demand, and may be willing to pay for, security.

Yet there is a gap between what they need and what they are able to command. To address this gap, we recently published a "Buyers Guide for Secure ICT."[2] This guide recommends questions that buyers can ask ICT suppliers to help them evaluate the security of the products and services that these suppliers deliver.

Despite best efforts, the reality of today's dynamic technological environment—with product cycles of 18 months or less—continues to challenge policy development. Two developments are dramatically altering the security picture.

First, we are moving to the cloud. We store our information there on virtual machines operated by major providers like Amazon Web Services. While AWS and Microsoft's Azure provide much stronger cybersecurity and resilience than any single enterprise can field, they also create systemic risk, with large potential consequences from technology failures or attacks.

A second emerging source of risk is the Internet of Everything (IoE). In a few years there will be ten times as many devices—Fitbits, heart monitors, automobiles, thermostats, machine tools, and floodgates—connected to the internet than today's smartphones and computers. These devices, when combined with 3-D printing, promise to disruptively transform manufacturing and transportation. They will also create a ubiquitous, global sensor network that will be communicating what is going on everywhere. And these sensors are shockingly insecure—built with easy to guess passwords, transmitting their data unencrypted, and being essentially un-patchable.

---

[2] "Purchasing Secure ICT Products and Services: A Buyers Guide," EastWest Institute, September 2016, *https://www.eastwest.ngo/sites/default/files/EWI_BuyersGuide.pdf.*

The conventional wisdom is that the IoE represents a massive increase in the attack surface. But at EWI, we are exploring two questions. First, why do we assume the bad guys will own the sensor network? Why not have the good guys own it and use the knowledge of what is happening on the internet to increase security—for example, by isolating problems and fixing them before they can spread? Second, we ask, how will the IoE shift the balance between endpoint and network security, and what are the societal implications of that shift?

One that is gaining currency in the United States is the Cybersecurity Framework created by the National Institute of Standards and Technology, or NIST, which is part of the U.S. Department of Commerce. The framework lays out the basics of a cybersecurity program that all firms should manage to. It also lays the foundation for future cyber insurance underwriting standards.

For at least a decade, there has been a lot of hype that we will all be left freezing in the dark, as was the case before the turn of the 21st Century with the so-called millennium or Y2K bug. These scenarios have not materialized, and in fact it is actually quite difficult to create broad systemic damage today. But the capability to attempt catastrophic attacks is increasing, and the generally deteriorating international security situation does not help.

In sum, it is a dynamic risk environment, augmented by our electronic connectedness and interdependence. We must continually adapt risk management to rapidly changing technology. Agility rules.

HOW SHOULD THE U.S. GOVERNMENT MOVE FORWARD TO MEET THESE CHALLENGES?

Over the past 8 years, the previous administration working closely with this committee and the rest of Congress, tested, revised, and eventually established a clear set of roles and responsibilities for cybersecurity among the relevant Federal agencies. One can trace the progress of these efforts that took place on a bipartisan basis across administrations and Congresses, including:
- Homeland Security Presidential Directive 23/National Security Presidential Directive 54, "Cybersecurity Policy," January 8, 2008.[3]
- The Comprehensive National Cybersecurity Initiative, May 2009.[4]
- The March 2013 "Bubble Chart" (See Attachment A).
- Six statutes enacted in 2014 and 2015——
  - National Cybersecurity Protection Act of 2014 (S. 2519), which codifies DHS's cybersecurity center.
  - Cybersecurity Enhancement Act of 2014 (S. 1353), which codifies the National Institute of Standards and Technology's (NIST's) role in cybersecurity.
  - Cybersecurity Workforce Assessment Act (H.R. 2952), which requires the DHS to develop a cyber-workforce strategy.
  - Border Patrol Agent Pay Reform Act of 2014 (S. 1691), which gives DHS new authorities for cybersecurity hiring.
  - Federal Information Security Modernization Act of 2014 (S. 2521), which reforms Federal IT security management.
  - Cybersecurity Act of 2015 (within H.R. 2029), December 15, 2015, which enhances protections for information sharing and further strengthen's DHS viila [sic] coordination role.
- Presidential Policy Directive 41, "U.S. Cyber Incident Coordination."[5]

These documents firmly cement the primary role of the Department of Homeland Security in securing the Nation's critical cyber infrastructure. In doing so, these documents are broadly consistent with each other and reflect two important assumptions:
- First, cyber space is fundamentally a civilian space. As former Deputy Secretary of Homeland Security Jane Holl Lute and I wrote in Wired in 2011, cyber space is "a neighborhood, a library, a marketplace, a school yard, a workshop—and a new, exciting age in human experience, exploration, and development. Portions of it are part of America's defense infrastructure, and these are properly protected by soldiers."[6]

This is an important assumption for two reasons. First and foremost, it is fundamentally consistent with American values. As a Nation, we have long recognized the importance of the military in providing the common defense, within limitations

---

[3] See, *https://fas.org/irp/offdocs/nspd/nspd-54.pdf.*

[4] Currently archived after partial declassification in 2011 at: *https://obamawhitehouse.archives.gov/node/233086.*

[5] See, "Presidential Policy Directive—United States Cyber Incident Coordination," July 26, 2016, *https://obamawhitehouse.archives.gov/the-press-office/2016/07/26/Presidential-policy-directive-united-states-cyber-incident.*

[6] See, "A Civil Perspective on Cybersecurity," *https://www.wired.com/2011/02/dhs-op-ed/.*

in tradition and law that respect the historical lessons learned when the Crown quartered soldiers in civilian homes without consent, after the actions taken to suppress the Whiskey Rebellion of 1794 with the authorization of Justice James Wilson, and, post-Reconstruction in the Posse Comitatus Act of 1878. This tradition is reflected in Department of Defense Directive 3025.18, "Defense Support of Civilian Authorities."

The appropriate role of the military in cyber space is also important from a practical standpoint. The military must protect its own assets and its ability to project force globally. It relies on a safe and secure cyber space to do both of those things. But simply as a practical matter, the Defense Department cannot secure all of cyber space. Indeed, as we have seen over the past 10 years, it is challenged to protect its own electronic assets and those of critical defense contractors from internal and external attacks. These jobs are too important to our National security to permit DoD to be distracted by other tasks that are in the end not part of its core mission.

- The second assumption reflected in current law and policy is that securing cyber space is a team effort. No single agency, and no single company or group of companies, can handle this challenge by itself. There must be cooperation and coordination. Agencies must work with each other and with the private sector, applying their capabilities and authorities in a seamless manner.

Seamlessness is not easy. In fact, in order to achieve it and avoid key problems falling through the cracks, there needs to be some overlap in responsibilities. While overlap can generate confusion, it is essential for full coverage.

These policy documents are explicit about the overlap, laying out joint responsibilities for tasks where appropriate. Such joint activities have become the norm in today's U.S. Government. Every morning, the Departments of Homeland Security, Justice, and Defense coordinate on a "First Look" video conference, sharing the latest developments and coordinating action plans. Conflicts can arise, for example, between the DHS mission to mitigate problems in critical infrastructure and the FBI's mission to preserve evidence for prosecution. These operational problems get worked out on the ground when these agencies work together with the victim of a cyber attack. And, when chronic or policy differences arise, a well-organized National Security Council will do its job and resolve those differences satisfactorily among the agencies for the good of the Nation.

CONCLUSION

Cyber space is a dynamic and dangerous environment. It is also the global endoskeleton of commerce, trade, and all manner of human interaction. Securing it, an essential task, is a global, multi-stakeholder effort that must bring all capabilities to bear in a cooperative manner. Agility rules. The United States is a world leader in having clearly established roles and responsibilities within Government so that it can play its critical role. The new administration and the Congress should focus on getting the implementation right.[7] Time is too short to do otherwise.

---

[7] As co-panelist Frank Cilluffo stated, "PPD–41 is a good initiative, but the real test will lie in the manner and nature of its implementation." See, "Overview and Analysis of PPD–41: US Cyber Incident Coordination," July 27, 2016, *https://www.lawfareblog.com/overview-and-analysis-ppd-41-us-cyber-incident-coordination.*

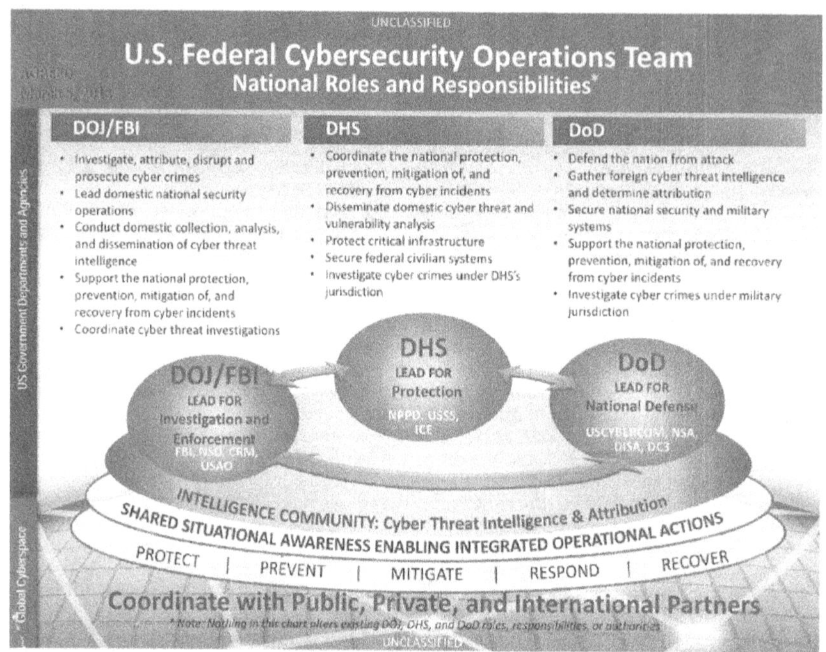

Chairman MCCAUL. Thank you, Mr. McConnell.

I will recognize myself for questions.

You know, I kind-of went through the litany of attacks, and they are—they have been very numerous. You know, North Korea on Sony Pictures, very destructive; Iran hitting the financial sector; to China stealing 20 million security clearances; to Russia interfering with our elections—and whether you are a Democrat or a Republican, that is an American issue, and the next time it could happen to the Republicans; and most recently, this—that alleged attack on the CIA, with some of the most sensitive cyber tools in the U.S. Government.

Yet, there never seems to be any consequences to this bad behavior. I have five children. If there aren't bad—if there aren't consequences to bad behavior, bad behavior continues.

The Chinese—I think we had a meeting with them after they stole the 20 million security clearances.

So my first question is to General Alexander. I mean, there are no rules of the game, as you mentioned. There are no consequences.

How do you see that? But also, importantly, how do you see the role between the military and the civilian counterpart, DHS, in terms of defending the Nation and also offensively responding?

General ALEXANDER. Thank you, Chairman.

I think the role is, first—I will start with the military side. The military's responsibility is to defend this country, in terms of offensive capabilities outside the country. If you think about an attack in cyber space, I look at that as FEMA and the military working together.

Do you have—whose responsibility would it be to work with State, local government, and industry to build back up damaged infrastructure? DHS has the lead.

DOD and the intelligence community should be going after the perpetrators of that or the country that is attacking us, because DOD's responsibilities would most logically go from cyber into the physical domain.

One of the reasons that we couldn't have Sony attack North Korea—while I think Sony could win, it could start a war on the Korean Peninsula, and that is a Government responsibility.

But here is where it gets tricky. I think there are several things that you need to put in place.

First, I agree with the organization around DHS of organizing NPPD and others into an agency. I think that makes sense.

I think you need to go further. I think you need to look at the civilian part of Government, look at the information technology and cyber. It is not sufficient. They don't have the resources; they will never get the people. Consolidate that in a disalike organization and put that under somebody.

That organization would be responsible for protecting Government. DHS would be responsible for protecting DHS and working with the rest of that, and could be responsible for protecting the rest of that Government.

When the Nation is being attacked like Sony, DHS, DOD, and DOJ should be notified through the same portal at the same time, and they should practice the rules of engagement. What is DHS going to do to help ensure Sony doesn't collapse, or the financial sector, or energy sector doesn't collapse? What is the Defense Department, the intel community, and law enforcement going to do to stop that attack?

My experience from being on the offense: The offense always wins because the defense is terrible.

We can fix the defense by getting Government and industry to work together. I think DHS should have the lead. I think we should bring in parts of the intelligence community and the military into those meetings to talk with industry so they know that this is an all-of-Government approach.

DHS could have the lead. We would call them the public face.

That is before Bruce came in. We would have changed the public face a little bit.

Just kidding, Bruce.

But if you think about it, we wanted DHS to be the public face for just the reasons that you said.

But industry wants to know: When I am being attacked by Iran is the military and the Government going to stop that attack while you help me fix this part?

That is where we have failed, in my opinion, and where we can take these next steps.

Chairman MCCAUL. I completely agree.

Last question to the remaining three witnesses—my time is very limited—is we passed the Cybersecurity Act. We will be providing oversight. This committee also intends to pass legislation to prioritize cyber within DHS to create a cybersecurity agency, taking the NPPD and making that a more prioritized, streamlined agency within the Department.

Do the three of you—and I think General Alexander has already answered that question—but do the three of you agree with this idea in principle?

Mr. DANIEL. Yes, Mr. Chairman. I think that taking NPPD out of being a headquarters function, which it is clearly not, and making it into a line agency within DHS, along with the other functions that DHS has, and prioritizing that makes a great deal of sense.

I think that continuing that holistic focus on our critical infrastructure and the Federal civilian agencies also makes a great deal of sense, and that would, I think, put DHS on an even more solid foundation to partner with the Defense Department and the Justice Department in doing their mission.

Chairman MCCAUL. Right.

Mr. CILLUFFO. Mr. Chairman, I would echo that. Not to be ingratiating, but I think this committee deserves a lot of credit for moving legislation in this space, and I think most notably some of your cyber bills.

I see three primary criteria. I mean, first DHS needs to get its own house in order, lead by example. Then it needs to administer with NIST and OMB and others, obviously the Federal civilian agencies, because the initiative, as General Alexander said, clearly does remain with the attacker, but some of these civilian agencies are even—are woefully behind some of the military capabilities are to defend.

Then I think it is really about enabling the most critical of our critical infrastructures. To me, I think if everything is critical nothing is critical. I am not taking away from 16 sectors, but I think we need to start really zeroing in on the four life-line sectors and the so-called Section 9 companies.

So I do feel you also need to streamline capability that the Department has for cyber crime efforts outside of NPPD. So I think there is a lot more that can be done, and I think an agency is a way to do it.

Chairman MCCAUL. Thank you.

Finally, Mr. McConnell.

Mr. MCCONNELL. Thank you, Mr. Chairman.

So yes, I agree with—it is always great to be on a panel where I can agree with Keith, so this is good for me.

I would say that we spent a lot of time while I was at Homeland Security debating what the name of this new organization should be. I think it is a low bar. Any name is going to be better than National Protection and Programs Administration, or whatever it is. So I think you should just get it done, sir.

Thank you.

Chairman MCCAUL. Thanks so much.

Chair recognizes the Ranking Member.

Mr. THOMPSON. Thank you very much.

I am glad to see the agreement on the role for DHS in this great challenge that we have.

One of the things that we are grappling with is some of the things that we are dealing with go to the basic threat of our democracy. My opening comments talked a little bit about Russia's involvement, and that involvement is very concerning because they have somehow looked at this as a vulnerability and have decided to take full advantage of it.

So—and I will start with you, General—have you given thought to what we should do to shore our vulnerability as a country, to defend our democracy and how we select our leaders?

General ALEXANDER. Yes. Ranking Member Thompson, I have talked to some of the States and I am going to meet with some of the States on just that issue to give them my thoughts and advice.

I think it is important to recognize we have got to fix our defense, and you sit in a key position that can help get our Nation on its feet, from a Government perspective, so that DHS, DOD, DOJ work together in that common cause, each with their roles and responsibilities, and ensure that they are well understood.

Then we need to educate the American people on cybersecurity, and we need to help build the bar—raise the bar for industry with the NIST Framework, incentives, and liability protection.

If we were to do those we would significantly improve the cybersecurity posture of this country.

Mr. THOMPSON. Well, and part of, I guess, my direction—and I will go to the other witnesses—if I hear you correctly, are you talking about some National system of election protection initiated by Congress?

General ALEXANDER. Not necessarily. It may be run by the States. I think the States have a responsibility here.

I think what Congress—what you can do here with this committee, and you have already done in part, is get things like the National Institute of Standards and Technology—they have a cyber framework. We recommend in the commission that you take that framework, make it metrics-based so it is something you can measure, and get people to apply that as a way of getting liability protection and a way of incentivizing.

Now, if you did that the States could do the same to the election process. That would significantly improve——

Mr. THOMPSON. Yes. But at some point somebody is going to say we can't afford it, you know, for whatever reason. I think what I am trying to get to is where our role as Members of Congress fall within—in this framework to guarantee that it occurs.

Would any of the other witnesses like to address that?

Mr. McConnell.

Mr. MCCONNELL. Thank you, Mr. Thompson.

I would say two things about the election situation. First, if it is true that defense is lousy—which I agree, and there are some things we can do about that—we also need to start figuring out how to manage the offense and try to cut the supply down, both through consequences and through self-measures of restraint.

On the election systems in the States, I think the underappreciated vulnerability here is with the companies who manufacture and support these election systems. They are not accountable at all. They do not make their machines available for inspection by security experts.

The DHS has designated election systems as critical infrastructure, but that does not necessarily apply in any way to the companies that support this.

In several Midwestern States the same company that prints the "I Voted" stickers also runs the so-called election management system for those States. So I think we need to take a look and bring the private sector into those, as well, sir.

Thank you.

Mr. THOMPSON. Mr. Cilluffo.

Mr. CILLUFFO. Congressman Thompson, I would like to actually look at the question a little different. Very valid question, but I think it actually stems from a point that the Chairman brought up in his first question, and that is we ultimately don't deter cyber; we deter actors from engaging in certain behavior.

Whereas the interference in the elections, rightfully so, generated headline after headline, the reality is is Russia's fingerprints have been on the mouse for a long time. This is not the first incident. It is a repeated pattern of behavior, including the first state-on-state cyber attack followed up by cyber weapons being used in concert of the battlefield in Georgia, as well as cyber and kinetic means in Crimea and the Ukraine.

So what I am really getting at is we can defend our way out of certain things, but ultimately we have got to start articulating a strategy that is aimed at dissuading, deterring, and, if need be, compelling bad behavior from occurring.

Russians are doing the same thing in France and Germany right now as we speak. So at the end of the day, we can get our systems secure; they are just going to find a new vulnerability. It is a cat-and-mouse issue.

So I think what we really need to do is get to the point where we are ready to impose cost on bad behavior.

We have been blaming the victim. We blame companies. We build higher walls protected with bigger locks after we get hit.

Imagine if all our homes were robbed and we called the locksmith. That is doomed for failure.

We have got to start leaning a little forward and looking at some proactive measures. I would argue that includes private-sector actions that can be taken short of hacking back.

Long-winded way of saying I think we need to actually start imposing costs on bad behavior.

Mr. THOMPSON. Thank you.

Yield back.

Chairman MCCAUL. The Chair recognizes Mr. Ratcliffe.

Mr. RATCLIFFE. Thank you, Mr. Chairman.

Appreciate all the witnesses being here today.

You know, when we talk about cyber challenges that we face today, clearly one of them is the cyber work force. All the members on this panel, we talk about creating jobs to grow the economy, but right now there are—estimates are somewhere in the neighborhood of 200,000 cyber-related jobs that are unfilled due to the lack of a qualified applicants to fill them.

While we would all, I know, love to solve that macro issue, I am going to focus specifically on what my subcommittee, the Subcommittee on Cybersecurity and Infrastructure Protection on this—on Homeland Security Committee, has jurisdiction and oversight over, and that is specifically the cyber labor work force issues at DHS.

So, General Alexander, let me start with you because at one point you had to manage the cyber work force at the NSA. So if instead of me sitting here this was Secretary Kelly, what advice would you be able to offer him—and you are smiling, so maybe you already have—about programs at the NSA or maybe even out in the private sector that he might be able to leverage to address that problem at the DHS?

General ALEXANDER. Yes, I was smiling because you said Secretary Kelly, and I was thinking, "John, what the heck were you thinking?"

[Laughter.]

General ALEXANDER. Actually, that is a great point. I think one of the things that we need to look at in DHS—there are so many political appointees and you have such a rotation, the stability of the work force at the management level is in shambles. People come in, they are a political appointee, they go for a while, and then they are out.

The difference at the National Security Agency and within the military are people are professionals brought up through that, and so the person who is running a cyber area has tremendous depth and experience in that, is recognized by the work force, has gone to school in it.

I think we need to look at that from a DHS—the number of political appointees. We have, you know, thousands of those. I just say for you that are working it, that is the first part.

The second, a good area that DHS and NSA actually work together in is on the cyber education. We actually go out and with universities we give them a curriculum and we certify it. It is certified by both DHS and NSA as a cyber curriculum.

I think bringing in students from that and incentivizing them to come into DHS—like NSA does; we get a tremendous amount out of that—is a good thing to do and you know they are already trained. That is a great population out there of kids that want to come in and work in this area.

I think I would look at both, and that is what I would tell Secretary Kelly.

Mr. RATCLIFFE. Thank you. You know, I think this is an important enough issue that I want to use my time to give all of the witnesses here an opportunity to weigh in on this.

Mr. Daniel, you—obviously your role as the special assistant to the President and cybersecurity coordinator for 4.5 years, I think I would appreciate your perspective on this, as well.

Mr. DANIEL. Certainly. Thank you.

I think to get at your question about the broader work force issues and the economy as a whole, I think one of the things that we are beginning to realize is that as we build these curriculums we actually have to think about the problem and break it down, that it is not just producing cybersecurity professionals, it is that we actually need to produce a variety of cybersecurity professionals and we actually need to start making sure that our curriculum and our training, you know, does provide a core for—that all professionals need, but then allow some specialization in there.

Are you going to be a hands-on-keyboard, you know, firewall defender? Are you going to be a hunter? Are you going to be, you know, a policy integrator, one that looks holistically at the problem?

Those are different skills sets, and we need to start building people that come out with those different skill sets because they are going to fulfill different roles in the ecosystem.

Specifically with respect to DHS, I—to me I actually see this as a broader problem of how we manage the tech work force and other specialized skills in the Federal Government as a whole. It is really about speed and flexibility.

One of the primary lessons that I learned from my time in the White House is we can get people to come into the Government for a while. They will take lower pay for a while. They just won't do it for their entire career.

So this idea that we are going to recruit kids out of college and bring them into one Federal agency, probably one bureau, and keep them there for 40 years and have them retire in their 60's, that is just ludicrous. That is not how any of the work force operates.

So we need to enable our Federal agencies to both bring people in faster and allow them to bring people in and out from the private sector with greater degrees of flexibility over the course of their career in order to allow for that rotation and that rejuvenation of the work force. I think that is the key factors of what we are going to need to get at in order to deal with the work force problems.

Mr. RATCLIFFE. Terrific. Thank you.

Frank.

Mr. CILLUFFO. Congressman Ratcliffe, I mean, I think Michael nailed it. Speed and flexibility, certainly from a civilian hiring perspective, and that is something some of the Title 50 or intelligence community entities can actually move a lot faster, and I think that is something perhaps DHS can look to.

Another issue, though, that just dawned on me is I had mentioned the attacks on Estonia, so I would bring my students—as a—representing a place of higher education, obviously I advocate the roles that universities play. But I also think there is a huge K–12 opportunity here, and when I go to Estonia you have first-graders and then you have got students that are going into their high school gymnasium with a STEM focus.

They are learning to speak Estonian, English, and code at first grade. First grade. I fear that we are going to be behind that work force power curve.

We know how to push all the buttons. We can make it look nice. But I feel like we really do need to get to some of that K–12 sets of issues.

And notably, women in STEM. It is not just—this is something that I think we are lagging and we really need to do more.

So work force generally, in terms of DHS it really is about speed and flexibility. Don't expect people to stay forever.

The Estonians also have what is called the Cyber Defense League. It is basically their active reserve component. They can pull the top people from industry to serve the government for a short period of time and then go back out, and they are all patriotic so it is basically like the reserve corps with a—active reserve corps with a focus on cyber. That is another area I think we can be looking at.

Mr. RATCLIFFE. Mr. McConnell, my time is expired, but if you can quickly answer?

Mr. MCCONNELL. Thank you, Mr. Ratcliffe.

Thank you, Mr. Chairman.

So the NSA programs that Keith mentioned are very good. Those authorities, hiring authorities are not always available at DHS, so you could look at that: Does DHS have the authorities to do what it needs to do?

It also has trouble with execution. NSA has a great program of getting summer interns in from colleges. They get those people a security clearance way before so they can come right in. They do that way up front. They have a finely oiled machine on that.

DHS is not so good at executing in that way. So I think you should set targets for DHS in this area and hold them to it.

Mr. RATCLIFFE. Thank you all.

Chairman, I yield back.

Chairman MCCAUL. Mrs. Watson Coleman is recognized.

Mrs. WATSON COLEMAN. Thank you, Mr. Chairman.

So it is clear that there is a consensus that China, Russia, Iran represent—and North Korea—represent our greatest threats. Do we have the capacity right now to prioritize who we need to give our greatest attention to? If so, would that be Russia?

Anyone.

General ALEXANDER. I can give it to you from my perspective. I think we can handle all—we can and have to handle all four because it is not clear how the threat will come back at us. We have to be prepared.

Mrs. WATSON COLEMAN. During the 2016 election obviously Russian government waged a campaign to undermine the U.S. democracy using hacked e-mails, WikiLeaks, and false news reports. President Trump has repeatedly praised Vladimir Putin and spent months denying that the Putin government carried out this campaign, accusing U.S. intelligence community of spreading falsehoods instead and suggesting that he will undo U.S. sanctions imposed against Russia.

Mr. McConnell, in your view, what message does the President's borderline-dismissive attitude toward this unprecedented attack on our democracy send to the Russian government as well as to other nations?

Mr. MCCONNELL. Thank you, ma'am.

You know, these attacks were predicted. A year ago General Clapper, the director of national intelligence, said, "Russia is assuming a more assertive cyber posture based on its willingness to target critical infrastructure systems and conduct espionage operations even when detected and under increased public scrutiny. Russian cyber operations are likely to target U.S. interests to support several strategic objectives, including influence operations to support military and political objectives."

These highly visible information and influence operations are new to Americans—except for one thing: Americans are also contributing to the degradation of the information space, usually for commercial or domestic political reasons. At the same time——

Mrs. WATSON COLEMAN. Mr. McConnell——

Mr. MCCONNELL [continuing]. We do have to keep talking to the Russians. The planet is getting too small to do otherwise.

Mrs. WATSON COLEMAN. So not disagreeing with anything that you have said, what message does this President's dismissive attitude communicate? Does it communicate a weakness? A coziness? A fearsomeness? Is it bold? Is it acceptable? Is it responsive? And is it proactive? What is it?

Mr. MCCONNELL. Well, ma'am, I never try to impute motives to other people. I think there are a couple different things here.

One is there is an on-going investigation, so I wouldn't want to comment on that.

I think it is important to remember that it doesn't do us any good to just vilify the Russians and push them into a corner. They don't respond well to that.

We have to figure out how to talk to them and engage with them, but at the same time, as you say, take them very seriously. It is a very serious threat to our country.

Mrs. WATSON COLEMAN. It doesn't seem like, according to what FBI Director Comey testified to, about they will be back and they really didn't care that we knew what they were doing, it doesn't seem that we are talking about having discussions with rational players here. It seems that we have a situation with an equally if not more arrogant regime that chooses to undermine our very democracy.

So my question to you, General Alexander: What are your thoughts on this?

General ALEXANDER. I think two sets of thoughts: First, we have to have consequences for somebody coming after our country, and I think the Chairman put that right. There have to be consequences and people have to know it.

We need to give the President and the Secretary of Defense latitude, though, in their strategy and their approach. I think this is where President Trump can actually be very good for us because he is negotiating how we deal with Russia in the future.

I think what Mr. McConnell said is right. If we vilify them and we keep them pushed out we are going to fight them. We agree that a war—and you would agree a war is not where we want to go. We have got to figure out how to set this right.

So I think there has to be consequences. I think we have to have that discussion and we have to be open to it.

Mrs. WATSON COLEMAN. Thank you.

General ALEXANDER. We don't have to like them.

Mrs. WATSON COLEMAN. Thank you, General. I think that this attack that we have experienced is a form of war, is a—was a form of war on our fundamental democratic principles.

One last question if I might, Mr. Chairman. That is to Mr. McConnell, because he speaks to the fact that the international laws are behind on these issues in addressing issues of this nature.

My question to him: In this climate, how do you think—do you think it is possible that we could have those kinds of, "conversations" and move into some agreement as to what is and what would not be allowed on the National stage—international stage? Thank you.

After that I yield back.

Mr. McCONNELL. Thank you, ma'am.

As I note in my written statement, there is some progress at the United Nations and in some companies in developing these rules of the road, but it is very slow.

One bright spot is a new global commission on the stability of cyber space, which is co-chaired by Secretary Michael Chertoff, and it has the mission to accelerate that work on rules of the road. It is nongovernmental, represents all the interests in all the countries, and is working on a fast track to propose rules that governments can agree to. The governments don't always follow the rules, but if there are no rules then there is nothing for them to follow.

Chairman McCAUL. That is well put.

Chair recognizes Mr. Donovan.

Mr. DONOVAN. Thank you, Mr. Chairman.

Gentlemen, thank you for attending here, and thank you for the work that you do in this very important area for our Nation's security.

Our Chairman laid out some of the things that this committee has done, some of the great work in this area. We are lawmakers, and every time we have a hearing I ask the experts—because we deal with scores of issues every day; you deal with this issue—what could we do as lawmakers that could help you and help DHS and help the people who are responsible for protecting our networks more so than we have done so far?

The Chairman laid out some of the great work we have already done. What would you like to see this committee, this legislative body, do to help protect our data, our information from our enemies even further than we are able to do now?

I just leave it open to each one of you to comment. Thank you.

General ALEXANDER. If I could just start, based on the commission, what we saw there, I think there are a few things that this committee has already started on but could reinforce. First, getting industry and the Government to look at the NIST standard for cybersecurity framework—add metrics in, but get that as a standard across Government and industry. There are so many out there right now you are hard-pressed to figure out which standard and how you are applying it.

The second is liability protection. How do we protect these companies that meet a certain standard from all the lawsuits that they get?

Third—it was brought up by the Ranking Member—this is—could be expensive, so how do we incentivize industry and individuals to actually take the next step?

In those three areas this committee and Congress could help. We could set that up and get this going.

You know more about tax incentives and stuff than I do, but that is where I think my discussions with the financial, energy, health care, and the rest of government—where I think this would really help.

Mr. DONOVAN. Thank you, General.

Mr. DANIEL. Congressman Donovan, I think the—I would agree with—well, first of all I would say that this committee has done tremendous work in moving the ball forward in the legislation that you have already done, and that—it has made a tremendous difference.

I would say that, for example, CTA couldn't really exist without the—some of the legislation that you have already put in place and the liability protections for information sharing, for example, that are already there.

I do agree with Keith that the—sort-of continuing to work on—we see a standard of care emerging in industry, but it is basically emerging via the courts and sort-of in a very ad hoc fashion, and I think getting—asking industry to step up and sort of proactively define what that standard of care is going to be would actually be very helpful to accelerate that process.

Then also, I think to Frank's point, continuing to refine the—and get the analysis done of what are the points where we—that we really care about in this country? Because yes, we can call an entire sector critical infrastructure, but that doesn't actually tell you where you need to prioritize within that sector.

Mr. DONOVAN. Thank you very much, Mr. Daniel.

Frank.

Mr. CILLUFFO. Congressman Donovan, let me echo everything that General Alexander and Michael Daniel said, and also thank you, because we hosted you for a talk on state and local cybersecurity, which I think is an area in particular to remember. The pointy end of the spear, it is always going to be—is always going to—it is not always going to be Federal. We need to ensure that our law enforcement and first responders writ large have some of the capabilities.

I think in addition to liability protection and in addition to allowing some of the information sharing, one thing I would like this committee to take a look at is defining some of the rules of the road for enabling active defense measures. I am not talking hack-back.

There is a lot of space between hacking back and building higher walls, and I think that there is some anxiety—in fact, I know there is—from the industry to be able to lean a little more forward until they felt like it was codified in some sort of way. So I think that would be a very valuable set of issues.

Then finally, this is more the appropriators, but policy without resources can be rhetoric. Let's make sure that we are funding the most critical of our critical infrastructure entities first and foremost.

Mr. DONOVAN. Thank you, Frank.

Mr. McConnell.

Mr. McCONNELL. Thank you, Mr. Donovan.

Three things: First, fix the DHS organization. Second, conduct oversight over DHS to make sure it does what it is supposed to do. Third, you might consider taking a look at the cyber insurance industry because it is now helping set the standards for what companies are going to do in their cybersecurity protection activity, and they are setting those standards, and they can be helpful to you, I think, and to the country in moving that forward.

Mr. DONOVAN. I thank you.

I thank all the witnesses for your input.

I yield back, Mr. Chairman.

Chairman MCCAUL. Thank you.

Chair recognizes Miss Rice.

Miss RICE. Thank you, Mr. Chairman. I just want to thank you for your opening statement about how this is not a Republican or a Democratic issue; it is an American issue. Because there was some questioning at the hearing the other day that I thought was, quite frankly, disgraceful—focusing on leaks instead of the—how important it is for us to make sure this doesn't happen again in the future.

Mr. Cilluffo, Russian cyber attacks on NATO targets rose by 60 percent in the last—in the past year, and cyber attacks against E.U. institutions rose by 20 percent. Members of NATO and the European Union are some of our closest allies, obviously, in the world, and those relationships are absolutely vital to our own security.

In your opinion, how do you think these allies will react to news that the Secretary of State will not be meeting with NATO foreign ministers next month but will instead be going to Russia later in April?

Mr. CILLUFFO. Yes. I don't know precisely how they will respond, but clearly it is important to recognize not only that NATO is a critical alliance to our trans-Atlantic relationship, but that our leadership visibly recognizes that, as well. So, I mean, Secretary Mattis has been very strong in terms of enhancing the—NATO's capabilities, and I hope we follow through on that.

One note to underscore, though, is we need to rethink our alliances. So we need NATO, of course. Five Eyes relationship is the strongest intelligence cooperative relationship in the world; we need that.

But we have other allies that aren't included in either of those. Where does Israel fit in? Where does Japan fit in? They have been on the front end of massive cyber attacks from North Korea of late as well as China, of course.

So I do think we need to rethink that a little bit.

Miss RICE. That is a good point.

Well, you also made the comment before that Russia is actually in France and Germany now, obviously, with these upcoming elections. What more should we be doing to aid our allies within NATO, the European Union, and even beyond, as you pointed out, to protect themselves from Russian cyber attacks?

Mr. CILLUFFO. That is a great point, and Admiral Rogers in those hearings earlier this week underscored that he is working directly with his signals intelligence counterparts in France and Germany. I think we need to continue to do that and move beyond, because quite honestly, we are only going to see bits and pieces.

We need the full snapshot of the activity we are seeing here, so this is something where intelligence relationships are dicey. They are—take forever to build and they could easily disappear based on relationships and what have you.

But I think in this particular case it would actually be pretty cool to pool all of that to see what other countries are seeing and then have a full snapshot of the activity we are seeing. Because history may not repeat itself, but it tends to rhyme, according to Mark Twain, and I think that is really right from a cyber perspective, too.

Miss RICE. I think you, in your opening statement or in one of the answers to one of your—one of the questions you kind-of put China and Russia together, and North Korea and Iran together. If you had to rank these four nation-states in terms of who would be the most dangerous in that order from most to least, and what are we doing to make sure that we are not—by focusing on whomever is the most, we are not allowing the least to kind-of get up the ladder?

Mr. CILLUFFO. That is a great question, and I am actually afraid that we chase shiny objects anyway, so—and then we get—our eyes are off the ball in other areas.

But here is the reality: Russia is the most capable. No question about that.

China, very active, mostly in computer network exploit, or espionage activity. Also building out their space and other sorts of computer network attack capabilities.

North Korea and Iran I am actually in some cases more concerned about because they are more likely to turn to computer network attack—massively disruptive attack. So capabilities differ, and intentions all matter. We have a responsibility to keep our eyes on the ball.

But North Korea in particular, I mean, it really is completely isolated. They have not only built out some of their cyber capabilities, they have got an army that includes officers operating in northeast China, southeast Asia, abroad, because they don't have a very connected country themselves.

But they are also turning to cyber crime. Normally criminals try to penetrate the state through corruption. Here you have a state penetrating organized crime to ensure the survival of the regime.

Miss RICE. This is my last question, with the Chair's indulgence, to all four of you—and this is just taking on—off on what you were just saying, Mr. Cilluffo. What more needs to be done in each of the 16 critical infrastructure sectors to ensure that the sectors remain operable even when they are under a successful attack?

Mr. DANIEL. So I can at least take a stab at that.

It is going to differ from sector to sector because the sectors are at different levels of maturity. Even within a sector, the difference between the very large players and the very small players is pretty radical.

But I think in many cases it is continuing to make cyber a priority within those companies and organizations at the Executive level; have them actually employ a risk-based approach; develop and test a response and recovery plan, so don't just have one on the shelf that the first time you open is when you have actually already had a problem, but actually develop it and test it ahead of time and make sure you have those relationships with law enforcement, with DHS going in ahead of time.

General ALEXANDER. If I could, I think what you need to do is—and you could help facilitate—you need to bring in the key executives from financial sector, five or six of those, with the energy sector, with health care, with the Government, and walk through exactly how we are going to do this: What they have to do, what they could do with incentives, how you could help, and what the Government response is going to be.

Because what you are asking is if Iran, who has attacked Saudi Arabia several times in the last 3 months, were to attack this country, we are not ready. So we need to get ready and we need to put that in place.

By having the industry players who are the most likely target walk through with Government how that is going to work and what you need to put in place, we would start down that road. We need to do that.

Mr. MCCONNELL. I can't disagree with those points. They are very good.

If I might go back briefly to your concern about NATO, I travel quite a bit in other countries, both to U.S. allies and adversaries. There is a lot of confusion across the board about what Americans' foreign policy is, and in particular in this area of information warfare.

I was recently at the Munich Security Conference with Chancellor Merkel and other foreign leaders, and there was much concern about where America is going on NATO. The Trump administration was there and said all the right things; there was a full-court press by the vice president, along with Secretary Mattis and Secretary Kelly, so that was very good. But there is a lot of skepticism still, a lot of concern, and I think the proof will be in the pudding.

Miss RICE. Thank you.

Thank you, Mr. Chairman.

Chairman MCCAUL. Thank you.

Chair recognizes Mr. Rutherford.

Mr. RUTHERFORD. Thank you, Mr. Chairman.

I thank the panel for being here today.

You know, it seems some of that confusion and disjointedness that we see in response to cyber attacks goes to exactly what Mr. McConnell said we really need to do earlier, and that is define the roles and response.

The bubble chart was an attempt at that maybe, but failed. I think, you know, when you say, "OK, DOJ is going to do the prosecution; DHS is going to do the protection; and then DOD is going to do the defense," it reminded me—you know, I am a 41-year law enforcement officer so I go back to the environment that I know well, and I know that that is kind-of the way it works in civil law in protection is, you know, law enforcement is the Government response to protect the public from the bad actors—whether they are criminal actors or even state actors, bad actors.

So I also understand this, though: Law enforcement are priority one response time. If you are the victim of an aggravated battery and an aggravated assault, we understand that there is like a 7-minute priority response time. So for 7 minutes that citizen better be able to deal with whatever it is on their own.

Our founding fathers understood that. That is why they gave individuals the 2d Amendment right to protect themselves.

There is a self-defense interest here, and it really concerns me when I hear people say, "Limit the ability to hack back." You are taking away the self-defense capability, I think.

Also, the general mentioned, you know, Sony could take them if you unleashed them. So I want to get back to this concept that we have to define the roles and response, because I think that is going to drive everything that we do from that point on.

Because I am really concerned about this idea that we are not going to allow Sony or some other corporation to defend themselves for that 7 minutes that we are waiting on law enforcement to show up. So how do you address that 7-minute response time the Government has to be able to protect our corporations from cyber attack?

General ALEXANDER. If I could start, light speed, in which the network operates, to go around the whole world once is——

Mr. RUTHERFORD. Oh, I understand that, but, I mean, there is a response time.

General ALEXANDER. Right. Now, so that is the problem that I see.

I agree with where you have taken this, but I would take it one step further, and that is we could be responding at network speed and should be, but we don't because we aren't organized to do that. We haven't looked at this as the common defense.

You hit the Constitution, and I think if our forefathers were here they would say the intent is when I am being attacked the Government is supposed to help me in certain things and I have to meet certain standards. My standard, let's call it the NIST; your standard is if Iran is attacking my you go kick their—and we will take it from here.

We don't have the ability today to do that. You have the organizational construct, and I think the bubble chart was a start. That is if you are—if a sector is being attacked the DHS has roles and responsibility to keep the Nation operating, DOD to go after these guys with cyber or any other element of National power.

So I would be concerned about a civilian corporation attacking back into North Korea and they assume it was our Government and it is an act of war and they lob missiles into Seoul. That could and would likely happen.

So you have to determine who is going to take the steps to do that. Now you are into the Defense Department and the President's roles.

So I would just offer that as consideration.

Mr. DANIEL. I think from—Congressman, I think from my perspective I think, you know, we worked very hard at the end of the previous administration to shape out the bubble chart into policy with respect to particular incidents, and that became Presidential Policy Directive 41, which I think actually helps clarify a lot of that—the roles and responsibilities and provides a very solid framework for enabling the Government to get its act together in terms of how we do response.

I would also hit on what Frank was saying, though, that there is a big—I agree with Keith that enabling a private corporation to go all the way back, there is also other problems, which is since the bad guys don't typically use, you know, computers and equipment labeled "bad guy stuff"——

Mr. RUTHERFORD. Right.

Mr. DANIEL [continuing]. They are, you know, commandeering— yes, they are commandeering, you know, third-party innocent people's machines and things like that. So we need to be very careful about, you know, how we go back at somebody.

But as Frank said, there is a big difference between simply building the wall higher and, you know hack-back. There is some space in there for companies to actually defend themselves.

But I think ultimately sort-of working out how we are going to do this and how we are going to divide up the roles and responsibilities between the private sector and the government—and governments; not just the U.S. Government but all governments around the world—and doing defense of their critical infrastructure is one of the fundamental policy challenges that we have right now. And how we are going to lay that out in some coherent framework that we can all live with I think is the policy issue that we are all struggling with.

I don't have a clear answer to that question right now, but I know that it is one that we have got to continue struggling our way through.

Mr. CILLUFFO. Congressman Rutherford, if I could just build on a couple of quick points: Seven minutes? It can be 7 years before the Government responds or it can follow up on some of the events that are occurring, so there is no 9–1–1 where you call and you get the Government to respond. So I think companies—I think it is an unfair playing field.

How many companies went into business thinking they had to defend themselves against Chinese intelligence services, or the SBR—Russian intelligence services, or North Korea, or Iran? Even the biggest companies in the world—for example, JPMorgan Chase, they spend $650 million a year on cybersecurity. They have well over 1,000 people focused on this particular issue. These are big numbers.

But no company—if you are throwing all-source intelligence, you see—cyber crime is getting so sophisticated that the lines between nation-state and criminal are narrowing dramatically, and they are blurring if they are using proxies. But here is the difference: Nation-states can use other forms of collection—signals intelligence, human intelligence, you name it. So that is an unfair playing field if you are a company.

So I am not asking to hack back, but I do think we should have suppressive fire. So there is one thing firing, there is another defending your own system from a suppressive fire perspective, if you want to use a military analogy in that respect.

So there is a lot more that can be done there. But don't——

Mr. RUTHERFORD. OK. I didn't catch that in your first comment about not hacking back, so that—I like that.

Mr. CILLUFFO. That is what I am for, so thank you.

Mr. RUTHERFORD. Good. Good.

Thank you, Mr. Chairman. I yield back.

Chairman MCCAUL. The Chair recognizes Mr. Correa.

Mr. CORREA. Thank you, Mr. Chairman.

Gentleman, a few weeks ago I asked a question from another panel and I am going to ask the same one here. I think I am beginning to get some responses or clarification.

My question then was how do you get private sector, public sector all to coordinate, and how do you get everybody to be accountable?

Let me explain. You just talked about JPMorgan. We know they are a hard target. But there are other players in the private sector, financially related, that are not spending millions of dollars to get hardened.

Same thing in the Federal Government—all levels of government, State governments. You mentioned—alluded to the fact that maybe there are some States out there that maybe aren't up to snuff on their election system. Probably there are some Federal agencies that are not as hardened as the CIA.

So the question is, how do you get everybody to coordinate?

Let me paraphrase what I am hearing from all of you, which is you gotta have standards—standards that address liability, which indirectly address cost, because everybody has got to share the costs if you are not—if you are going to protect yourselves. If you are going to get insurance of some sort here to protect yourselves you have gotta have some oversight, meaning some coordination.

Maybe that is the role of DHS, in terms of making sure everybody is talking to each other.

Mr. Rutherford talked about retaliation. Well—and response times. As you said, this is speed of light, so maybe that is where DHS assures that the government and others are there to maybe lay down fire suppression.

So this is a map here that maybe the role of DHS is really to coordinate private and public sector, not in the sense of managing it but to make sure everybody is talking to each other, to make sure that we have the response, to make sure we protect everybody in our critical areas, and maybe also look at working with our allies overseas, NATO and some of the others.

Open it up for comment.

General ALEXANDER. I will give you a first one, Congressman Correa, and that is I think when you look at this that we do have to walk through the roles, responsibilities, and the standards that we are going to have people at. We pushed to have the NIST framework as the standard, and I think we should look at that.

I think when you think about the relationship of DHS and DOD, the idea of having this done as an exercise here in Congress, where you could bring in first the Government and then other civilian agencies, would really pay dividends because we talk by each other. Words matter.

For example, if you look at missiles coming into the United States, you are going to want NORAD to shoot down those missiles. NORAD has to have the authority and the ability to do that in time to block the missile.

Now, they may not be 100 percent effective. A missile may come in and hit somebody.

DHS has now a role to help build that back up. It has protection and certain standards.

In cyber it is very much the same. I see a role and responsibility for DHS working with industry on these standards, but not being the portal for saying what DOD would do, but rather that is going to be a Presidential decision on the roles of, when do you respond and how do you respond? I think they should establish those and make that clear, and then show how you are going to have DHS, DOD——

Mr. CORREA. But to a certain level you have to have those rules up front——

General ALEXANDER. That is right.

Mr. CORREA [continuing]. Because you have got to respond in a nanosecond.

General ALEXANDER. That is right. We don't. We should. We don't have the rules and we should have them.

Mr. CORREA. Thank you.

Mr. DANIEL. So, Congressman, I think that—to build out a little bit of what you were saying, I think part of this is that one of the things that we are struggling with is that we operate at a scale that is very difficult to comprehend.

This was actually driven home to me when we did a joint exercise with the United Kingdom and their financial sector, and I realized that the entire United Kingdom financial sector—representatives of that could fit in this room, that you could literally get all of them together around the table.

We have 13,000 financial sector companies, roughly. So there is no way to, you know, sort-of do it by traditional sort-of organizational means.

That means to my mind sort-of two things. One is that we actually need to set up the structures to enable us to sort-of, if you will, use trees and other ways to get at that organizational problem so it is not DHS trying to talk to—or even NSA or anybody in the government—trying to talk to 13,000 institutions, Treasury talking to 13,000 institutions simultaneously. So we need some intermediate structures in there to help with that.

But then we also need to use the networks and the power——

Mr. CORREA. Standards?

Mr. DANIEL [continuing]. Power—yes.

Mr. CORREA. DHS-generated or standards of private sector?

Mr. DANIEL. I think private-sector standards, but I think when I——

Mr. CORREA. OK. Be like accounting rules.

Mr. DANIEL. Yes. Like Keith says, I am a big fan of the NIST Cybersecurity Framework. I also agree it needs metrics behind it to help organizations figure out how to actually apply the framework.

But clearly we need to be using network technology and I.T. technology to actually work for us in this space rather than just only against us in this area and allow us to use the network to communicate defenses at network speed. That is a large part of what we are trying to build toward right now, but I think that is going to be the only way that we get at these questions.

Mr. CILLUFFO. Just to build on some of those quick points, I do think standards are important, and I think that many of those can be driven by the private sector since they know their systems' vulnerabilities and capabilities better.

But let me just say two things. First—and it is not to go back to an old point, but if everything is critical nothing is. I think we have got to get—at least get to a grade B on the most critical of our critical infrastructures. These are our lifeline sectors. Think electric power and energy; think telecommunications; think financial services; and think transportation.

Let's start there because they are—a disruptive or destructive attack to any of those, the impact upon our economy, on our public safety, our National security could be incredibly damaging. So let's start it with those very initial points.

Then I think there are some systemic risks that we need to ameliorate or backfill some of those vulnerabilities. So, for example, I didn't bring it up in my remarks but in my written testimony I mentioned the SWIFT hack, which, by the way, North Korea is seen as a prime perpetrator.

But what made the SWIFT hack of last year—February of last year, and this was against the Central Bank of Bangladesh—unique was not that $81 million was stolen. That is bad. Bad day for the bank; bad day for its customers and clients. But the economy could absorb it.

What was important about that is it identified a systemic risk. The whole global financial institutions all are based upon that SWIFT. It clears billions—hundreds of billions of dollars daily. So to me that is a systemic risk. That rises above the noise.

If you look at the Russian attacks on the energy grid in the Ukraine, these are the sorts of—it was the first time a cyber attack had a physical consequence in a real-world environment. That is a big deal.

We are talking about the interference in the elections. Yes, big deal. I am actually worried about safety. That is a bigger deal, that you are taking off—if you don't have power I don't care what other critical infrastructure is up and running, we are not moving.

One in particular that is critical but so far behind in its security are water. So water is truly critical, but they are nowhere near the gold standard of the financial services sector.

My last word, enable organizations like the Cyber Threat Alliance. I highlighted the FSR, which are all the big banks that are coming together. These are the groups and organizations that are going to drive change, and I think historically there has been a little bit of arrogance that the Government thinks, "Government lead, private sector follow."

I take an opposite approach. I think private sector is going to lead and Government need to lead by example by doing—getting its own houses in order.

Chairman MCCAUL. Gentleman's time is expired.

The Chair recognizes Mr. Fitzpatrick.

Mr. FITZPATRICK. Thank you, Mr. Chairman.

Just a segue from Mr. Correa's question, focusing first on the Federal agencies. So there are two agencies, DHS and the FBI, that have concurrent jurisdiction over cyber crime investigations.

My first question is: Have you encountered any issues with that as far as overlapping jurisdiction, redundancy?—would be my first question, because that is an issue in the law enforcement community.

Second, the relationship between—since this is the Homeland Security Committee—DHS and the private sector, because I think most of us know that typically the private sector is far ahead of the curve over the Government when it comes to, typically, matters of I.T. and technology.

Is there any proactive outreach steps that DHS has done for any of your organizations to reach out and try to learn from what you all know?

Mr. MCCONNELL. If I could just start on that, sir, on the private-sector part, one of the reasons that we all agreed on the bubble chart when we were serving in the Government was because DHS does have a good interaction with the private sector of exchange of information and coordination. So they can improve on that, but it is a good—as General Alexander said, a good public face in that area.

The larger point that you made also makes a lot of sense, and I leave that to my other colleagues.

Mr. DANIEL. So I think that the—Congressman, I think the question of, you know, the proactive steps that DHS has taken, you know, certainly, yes, you can see the programs that they are trying to put in place, like the Automated Indicator Sharing Program, the teams that they have developed to go out and assist upon request, the critical infrastructure protection efforts that they have to engage proactively—all of those are good elements and I think they need to continue to be resourced and expanded and prioritized, as Frank says, to focus on the most critical areas.

I think that those are critical to continue.

I certainly think that your question on the concurrent jurisdiction is one that clearly warrants some further discussions. My personal view is that DOJ and DHS, in the form of FBI and Secret Service, have worked out a way to handle that in most cases, and it is—they actually cooperate better than sort-of some of the public perception would lead you to believe sometimes.

But that is still something that should probably be reevaluated every so often as we look at what the responsibilities of all of those agencies are.

General ALEXANDER. I can give you my experience working with the FBI and Secret Service on this. The FBI was great to work with for us, and we had an assumption between Director Mueller and myself, and that was any cyber action would be a law enforcement because most of the things that we are seeing are criminal in nature, and he would have the lead. If it turned out to be a nation-state then those would turn and we would support him, in terms of the law enforcement.

I think between Secretary Napolitano, Secretary Gates, Mueller, myself, and the bubble chart, we actually had pretty good agreement across how we were going to do each of those.

I do think that we should look at how we organize our Government, and is this what industry would do for organizing cyber, and having it in three pillars and separated all out the way we do. We do that in part because of all the issues with civil liberties and privacy and the public faces and that, but if we were running our Government like a company would we run it this way?

I just ask that because you have asked and you gave some great points, and the answer is, "Nope, we wouldn't do that."

Here is part of the reason. We have talked about people. If you were in charge of all three and you put them together would you share more of those people amongst them to make sure we could each do our job? Yes. Would we work together better? Yes. How could we get there and what should we do?

Secretary Gates and Napolitano had some great discussions on that. It might be good for you, Chairman, to bring those in because I think it actually answers some of the questions you are asking, Congressman, and they are better at that than I was.

Mr. FITZPATRICK. Thank you. I yield back.

Chairman MCCAUL. Just for the record, are you saying that it should be more integrated and less siloed—those three?

General ALEXANDER. Yes, Chairman, I am. I think it should be more integrated.

Chairman MCCAUL. I think that is a——

General ALEXANDER. I agree with civilian control. I think you can look at—Secretary Gates came up with this approach to say, why don't we work to have some strategy to bring those together so that we all benefit from the talent?

Chairman MCCAUL. Yes. I tend to agree.

Chair recognizes Ms. Jackson Lee.

Ms. JACKSON LEE. Let me thank the Chair and the Ranking Member for again being at really the cutting edge of securing this Nation, and that is the issue of cybersecurity, which a decade ago I—the most we might have been saying, General, is that 85, 87 percent of the cyber world was in the private sector. That was the mantra or the conversation, and it was considered infrastructure, and we looked at it in those terminologies.

But I am glad that we are looking now to prioritize cybersecurity, protecting the cyber system. But more importantly, I want to thank all of the witnesses for their focus on the importance of the Department of Homeland Security.

I am excited about a potential reserve corps—vetted individuals that move in and out of the corporate community on the basis of public service. I might make the point that because of Mr. Snowden I would prefer those individuals who—forgive me—are not contract, you don't know where they are; they are sitting right at DHS working with us.

I applaud the zero to 12—I guess I am already on the birth, but let's go from K to 12. I don't mind doing zero to 12, start talking early about STEM, but the—that is OK. The K to 12 I think is an excellent idea, and I also think it is important to develop that base of informed professionals ready to be on task to be on the offense.

So let me ask questions related to some of the public incidences that we have been seeing. I want to start with General Alexander and Dr. Cilluffo, if I can.

Last week's Justice Department indictment of two Russian government agents in the Kremlin's cyber division is a watershed moment in our efforts to counter state-directed cyber hacking campaigns. What does last week's unsealed indictment regarding the 2014 Yahoo breach tell us about the Russian government's 2016 election interference, and does this give us a better understanding of the importance of attribution? Because you all had talked previously about getting right to it, not being shy about who has done it, and if you would answer that.

Let me add to that, to General Alexander, very quickly, your exit memo indicated—and I have other questions but I am going to yield for you all to answer—indicated your work with the NSA and Cyber Command the greatest privilege and honor of your life. You also described NIST and Cyber Command employees as people who dedicated their lives to protecting the Nation—not for money, but for the mission.

What do you think about how troubling it is to have seen the President compare the I.C. to Nazi Germany and denigrate the contributions of your former colleagues? What, if any, effects could any President's attacks on the intelligence community have on our analysts, our relationships with the allies, and the work of the I.C. in recruitment?

But, General Alexander and Doctor, if you could go to the first question that I asked, please?

General ALEXANDER. Could you say that first question again? I was thinking about that second one. Could you just quickly say the first——

Ms. JACKSON LEE. No problem at all. It is to comment on the indictments of the Russian agents regarding Yahoo and to—what does the breach tell us about Russian government's interference in 2016? Then the subset of that: Does this give us a better understanding of the importance of attribution?

Then you could go into the other one, and then I will yield to the doctor.

General ALEXANDER. Yes. So on attribution—I will start there—absolutely vital. It is something that we jointly worked about 12 years ago starting getting attribution and have gotten much better at it.

What this shows me—from what we are seeing on Russia, on Yahoo, on our elections, on China—is our defense is terrible, and we don't have any consequences. I agree with the way the Chairman said that. We have to have consequences.

I think we need a two—at least a two approaches to this. Come up with the consequences—think of that as rules of engagement; and then go fix the defense by getting industry and the Government to work together.

I agree with Frank saying the Government should be the standard. We should set the standard for the rest of the Nation.

With respect to working at NSA and the comments about the employees of the intelligence community and others, I would go back to my time in NSA. You know who really did a great job coming up there was President Bush.

He came up and talked to the people about what they were doing and he made this comment to us, and it was the most important leadership thing that I saw in 40 years, and it was to me he said, "Look, you protect the Nation, I will take the heat." He told the people of NSA, "You are here to protect the country," and they—he made them feel good.

We need leaders to make people in Government feel good about what they are doing.

Ms. JACKSON LEE. Thank you.

Mr. CILLUFFO. Congressman Jackson Lee, I—you know, I think that the indictment was quite startling. To actually see what we have all kind-of known, that you have a nation-state and that you have FSB officers turning to well-known—including someone who is on the world's most-wanted list, from a U.S. perspective, for cyber criminals—to do their bidding.

So we have know that any country worth their salt is going to work through a proxy because they don't want the muddy footprints coming back to them, or the cyber footprints. So I do think that it is a pretty big deal.

I think that the bigger takeaway, though, is it is just reflective of what they have been doing for a long time. The interference in the election, that is not new. This is what Russia has been engaged in for quite some time.

The one thing I would just caution everyone with is it is not just Russia. I mean, the perpetrators are vast. So what I don't want to do is focus all of our efforts on one actor when all the other actors are going to take advantage of that situation.

So I do find the indictments important. In the past we indicted PLA officers from the Russian—I mean from the Chinese army. People said, "What is the likelihood of them ever seeing a courtroom?"

Nil. But it sent a message. It signaled we mean business. Oh, by the way, these officers can't travel anywhere that has extradition treaties with the United States.

So it has some effect, and I am happy the indictments just did what they are supposed to do. Just the facts, ma'am.

Ms. JACKSON LEE. Thank you.

Chairman MCCAUL. Gentlelady's time has expired.

Mrs. Demings, from Florida, is recognized.

Mrs. DEMINGS. Thank you so much, Mr. Chairman and Ranking Member.

To all of our witnesses, thank you so much.

Mr. MCCONNELL. after the 2015 attack on Ukraine's electrical grid DHS and NCCIC was able to help the Ukrainian government respond to the incident. In your perspective, how well-positioned is the U.S. Government or the U.S. Government continue to be to help our European allies, including France and Germany, whose elections are being targeted by regimes like the Putin regime?

Mr. MCCONNELL. Thank you, ma'am.

Yes, I think that is still a work in progress. There is good coordination at the operational level between the NCCIC and their counterparts in most European countries, but the coordination at the policy level has a lot left to be done, and I think that is a really good question for you all to be asking about.

On the NATO side there is also very good collaboration in this area, so I think that the—in general that we are in a pretty good position to help them from lessons learned, and there has been quite a bit of conversation between the Europeans and the Americans post election and sharing some of the lessons learned.

Mrs. DEMINGS. Thank you.

The next question is for any of the witnesses. What concepts or principles are you hoping to see reflected in President Trump's Executive Order on cybersecurity, and are there specific policies or relationships that you would like to advise the President not to disturb?

Mr. DANIEL. Congresswoman, I can certainly start with that. I think that the principles that I would hope to see and the approach are actually what you—what we have certainly seen in some of the—in some of the versions that have made their way out into the public in the sense of continuing to emphasize the risk-based approach to cybersecurity, that you are not going to be able to protect everything all of the time, to continue the focus on moving a lot of the cybersecurity mission out of the hands of the—all of the Federal civilian agencies but leaving them—retaining accountability for protecting their information. But indicating that they don't have to be doing all of the protecting themselves and, you know, finding ways to do shared services across the Federal civilian side. That is incredibly important.

I think continuing to emphasize this—the fact that all of this has to be done, as we have all been talking about this morning, in partnership, that no one element within the Federal Government, no—the Federal Government by itself, and indeed, the United States by itself cannot tackle this problem, but we have to do it in partnership both, you know, within the Government, between State and local governments and the Federal Government, internationally, and with the private sector.

General ALEXANDER. I think three things that need to come out: One, we talked about fixing Government—I.T. and cybersecurity—and make that a standard, because right now when you look at it compared to industry it is way behind.

The second is we have got to have Government-industry collaboration and we have got to encourage that collaboration. I think we have got to also—a third point is figure out how we are going to protect critical infrastructure and where do you start?

I agree with what Frank said in terms of picking your starting points, but I think as a Nation we have got to go beyond. I think it is got to be: How do we educate the people? How do we take the next steps in terms of getting this collaboration? What can other sectors do while we focus on the lifeline, as Frank put it?

So we have got to cover that, and I would hope that is in there.

Mr. CILLUFFO. Just a couple of very quick points, and I think they have been raised here in different sorts of ways.

First thing I would do is to Mr. Rutherford's comment earlier: Clarify roles and missions of various agencies and entities and recognize that as much as we have been talking on the defensive side here, the reality is we are never going to firewall our way out of this problem. We have to be comfortable discussing some of our offensive capabilities because that leads to a cyber deterrence strategy.

We can't deter if the enemy doesn't know what capabilities we have. As the old movie, "What good is having the doomsday machine if no one knows you got it?"

So the reality is is I feel we need to look at it in a much more strategic kind of way, where we start clarifying roles and missions; we are comfortable about some of our capabilities; we articulate and, more importantly, demonstrate a deterrent capability; we manage what we can from a risk-based perspective.

I think that based on what I have seen I am pleased to see that the Trump administration is building on the continuity of what worked well in the previous administration, and then recognizing a couple of areas where they want to go a little further.

So I think for starters it is that roles and missions piece.

The one thing I would just caution is—I mean, an Executive Order is basically a statement of intent. That is where you guys come in is when do you codify some of those intentions and align that from a legislative perspective? I think you guys have honestly done a terrific job, and this committee, I think, more than any other committee is moving legislation.

Those are my quick thoughts.

Mrs. DEMINGS. Thank you very much. I am out of time.

Thank you, Mr. Chairman.

Chairman MCCAUL. Thank you.

Chair recognizes Mr. Langevin.

Mr. LANGEVIN. Thank you, Mr. Chairman. I want to thank you and the Ranking Member for organizing this hearing.

I certainly want to thank our distinguished panel of witnesses here, your testimony today and the many contributions you have made in moving the Nation's cybersecurity defenses forward and putting us in a much stronger place.

I have been at this cybersecurity issue, like the Chairman, now for the better part of a decade, and I certainly always feel as much as I have learned I still have so much more to learn. I certainly do when I have the caliber of a panel like you all here before us. So thank you for that.

General, I will start with you, and I thank you for your many years of service to the Nation and appreciate the work that you and I have done over the years on cyber. But in your written testimony you State, "However, the reality is that commercial private-sector entities cannot practically be expected to defend themselves against nation-state attacks in cyber space." I certainly completely agree with that.

However, most breaches—and I have heard numbers anywhere from 85 percent upwards of 95 percent—are not sophisticated but rely on unpatched systems, poor—a poor understanding of network topography, or other examples of poor cyber hygiene. So how can we increase the signal-to-noise ratio so that the Government can focus on protecting against nation-state attacks?

For the panel, I would certainly be interested in your perspectives on why so many breaches continue to be the result of failures and—forgive me for using the term—cyber hygiene?

My second question—and I certainly would welcome the panel on this, as well—is for Mr. Daniel. Thank you for your work at the White House. Certainly in my time there—your time there when General Alexander was there you both were incredibly accessible to me and very helpful.

So to Mr. Daniel, I know you spoke at the Cybersecurity for a New America conference on Monday, and I had the chance to review some of your remarks. One thing that really leapt out at me was your discussion of where an organization should spend their marginal dollar on defense.

So this ties in with my interest on cybersecurity metrics. You know, how can we tell whether our controls are working? Same thing that goes with just adopting the NIST standards. You know, what organizations are adopting them, and to what degree are those standards even effective?

So what suggestions do you have—and I would, again, invite the panel to chime in—to allow us to better understand where that marginal dollar should be spent?

So, General Alexander, if we could start with you?

General ALEXANDER. Congressman, good to see you again.

I would say first we have got to have standards. In order to set those standards we have talked about the NIST and the NIST framework, but I think we have to take a couple more steps.

When you look at what goes on, the big companies can afford to throw money and resources at it. Your small and mid-sized don't have the resources, don't have the money, can't afford it, and so they are in a risk calculus: Can I absorb a hit? They are in the feeder tank, so think about what happened to Target and the air-conditioning company.

So when you look at those things, how do we set up and incentivize this? That is where Congress can come in.

I think we need to set the standards. I think we need to incentivize them for having those standards.

You can look at it by sectors and you see the SEC and the New York Department of Financial Services are already setting standards in cybersecurity.

I think Congress has a role in that. What is the initial standard and how do we do that?

I think we have got to incentivize and therefore push the cybersecurity industry to come up with practical solutions for small, mid-sized, and large companies. I think the cloud and where this is going is going to play a large part in it. That is something we could talk about after.

Thank you.

Mr. DANIEL. Thank you, Congressman Langevin. It was always a great partnership that we had, and I always appreciated our conversations in this area.

I think from my perspective what I was alluding to there is that we have tended to focus on the cybersecurity industry on a very narrow slice of the problem and sort-of that "protect," maybe into the "detect" portion of the NIST Cybersecurity Framework.

But in many cases you now have chief information security officers and others buying new appliances and equipment and they don't really understand how it all fits together and they don't have a holistic view of what that "nth" device in their stack actually gets them, in terms of additional cybersecurity protection.

It may well be the case that for many organizations rather than buying the new shiny object or the newest technology, what they actually need to invest in is very solid recovery capability, and that might actually provide them more benefit down the road.

But I think part of this is that, again, you have to come at this from a holistic standpoint—not just the mechanics of the cybersecurity and the technology, but understanding how your work force interacts with it, how it interacts with your business processes, what are the impacts on your business economics, and come at it from that much more holistic standpoint.

Until we get to that point where we are actually making security the easier path—being cyber-secure the easier path to do rather than the harder path, people just aren't going to do it, or at least not enough people are going to do it at the scale that we need them to.

So I do think that there is a burden on the cybersecurity industry to step up to that, but also organizations to think more holistically about their cybersecurity and manage it as a risk, just like the manage their legal risk and their customer risk and other reputational risk and all the risks that they face as an organization.

Mr. LANGEVIN. Thank you.

Other panel members?

Mr. McCONNELL. It is great to see you, sir, and thank you for all your work in this area for so long.

I would just make one point on your comment about cyber hygiene and why it is still the biggest source of attacks and vulnerabilities. I think this approach we have today of telling people to patch their devices and get that latest patch in and don't click on attachments—bad attachments—doesn't work.

It is certainly not going to work when we 10 times as many devices attached to the network, and now I forgot to patch that lightbulb and it is now a—connected to the internet and is a vulnerability.

So I think there is going to be a shift in the industry moving away from the devices and the end-points more to the network layer and that the enterprise network operators and the tier one ISPs are going to have to take more responsibility for the security of the traffic that is coming over, and we can't leave it to the—to local cyber hygiene.

That is still important. We still have to secure those devices, but there has got to be a shift of responsibility if we are going to do this at scale.

Mr. LANGEVIN. Thank you.

Mr. CILLUFFO. Congressman Langevin, let me also thank you for all your terrific work in this space, and I have had the privilege of working with you for a number of years now.

Two things, though, that I would just build on. I agree with everything, although I would say to Bruce's point, still make sure you update all your patches and you don't click on bad links.

But yes, the vast majority of breaches are due to social engineering, including the most sophisticated. That is where human—other means, from an all-source collection standpoint, can be thrown at you.

Two things though: One, technology will continue to change; human nature is pretty consistent. So if you start looking at it from a behavioral standpoint there are certain things you can put in place. None of us discussed on this—on the panel here today the insider threat, which I still think is probably at the very top of the threat, agnostic to their ideological motivations or intentions.

Two things that I think will be—machine learning and A.I. There is a lot of buzz. There is a lot of gobbledygook, but there are some very real initiatives here, and I think the Department of Homeland Security deserves some credit here in terms of leaning forward with some of the STIX–TAXII opportunities, which enable more real-time cyber intelligence sharing.

I also think that, given your work on the Armed Services Committee, maybe we ought to be looking at some of the DOD acquisition cybersecurity components for the most critical of our critical infrastructure. In other words, it is looking from a supply chain perspective.

So Bruce brought up the point, I mean, small—even small banks, they don't have the resources the big financial institutions have. They have to collect that.

So they are either going to go through their providers, whether it is ISP or otherwise, but maybe there is another way to be looking at it where we start baking security on the front end and we have acquisition processes for some of these entities that ask, at least, the cyber question.

Mr. LANGEVIN. All great points, yes.

Thank you all.

I yield back.

Chairman MCCAUL. Let me thank the panel. What an excellent discussion. Very insightful, educational.

I do want to mention during the course of this hearing it has been reported there is a terrorist attack in London at the—both the parliament and Westminster Bridge. One confirmed dead and possibly 10 injured, and so we pray for those victims and Godspeed.

With that, other committee Members may have questions. This will remain open for 10 days.

This hearing stands adjourned.

[Whereupon, at 12:17 p.m., the committee was adjourned.]

APPENDIX

QUESTIONS FROM CHAIRMAN MICHAEL T. MCCAUL FOR KEITH B. ALEXANDER*

Question 1a. While the goal, for combatting cyber crime, is to make it financially untenable to conduct illegal activities, what would the corollary of this goal be for nation-state actors?

Answer. The goal for combatting nation-state actors is to deter them from engaging in activities that are particularly harmful to our National security, including destructive cyber attacks, massive theft of private-sector intellectual property, and access to critical infrastructure systems.

Question 1b. How do we tip the scales so that it isn't worth it for nation-state actors to break into our systems both in the private sector and in the Government?

Answer. Though some level of espionage is unavoidable, we must significantly improve our defense and the public-private partnership. Nation-states have long sought access to one another's secrets and will almost certainly continue to do so. Our company and Government networks are too easy a target for both nation-state and non-nation-state actors, especially when they stand alone. We need to significantly raise the bar and have an integrated "common" defense.

We need to treat the cyber realm more like the physical world when it comes to deterrence and having nation-states recognize that there are very real costs to acting against the United States in cyber space.

Question 2a. At the hearing, we heard that we need to rethink how the Government and private sector relate to one another on cyber issues.

What are your recommendations for rethinking the relationship between public and private sectors?

Answer. The key to rethinking the relationship between the public and private sectors on cyber issues is recognizing that for too long, we assumed that the private sector can largely protect itself on its own. Unlike in any other domain, we expect companies to protect themselves against nation-states, criminals, and script kiddies alike when it comes to cyber space; in the physical world, we certainly do not expect corporate America to deploy surface-to-air missiles to defend against nation-state bomber threats. Recognizing this dichotomy and taking steps to address by sharing much more detailed threat information in both directions, building interoperable defensive systems, exercising how the Government and the private sector would respond to a real, on-going threat, and establishing clear roles, responsibilities, and rules of engagement would be a strong first step in the right direction.

Question 2b. How do we ensure the private and public sectors can work together harmoniously, without overstepping the Government's role or creating a new regulatory regime?

Answer. It is critical that the Government and the private sector recognize their respective roles and responsibilities, and perhaps most importantly, their own capabilities when it comes to working together in cyber space. The Government must have a clear understanding of the roles and responsibilities of each department. Further, putting in place specific laws and stringent regulations are not particularly useful when it comes to a fast-moving technology area like cybersecurity because they are not very flexible and adaptive. The Government should set broad goals and encourage behaviors through positive incentives rather than through regulations and penalties. At the same time, both the public and private sectors need to rebuild the trust and confidence with one another.

---

*Gen. (Ret.) Keith B. Alexander is the former Director, National Security Agency and the Founding Commander, United States Cyber Command. Currently, he is the President and CEO of IronNet Cybersecurity and recently completed service as a member of the President's Commission on Enhancing National Cybersecurity.

Finally, we need to train how we are going to defend, first within the Government, and then between the Government and private sector. We should have routine drills to practice and build up our competence in responding to threats.

Question 2c. How can we ensure this much-needed and strengthened collaboration is nimble enough to consider the evolving nature of cyber threats and organizational needs?

Answer. Many of the regulatory and legal tools available to the Government are not particularly nimble. Positive incentives are most likely to achieve successful results in a dynamic threat and defensive environment. Similarly, flexibility on key policy issues and seeking to find the reasonable middle ground, rather than taking extreme positions on both sides of the debate on Capitol Hill and in Silicon Valley, are likely to reach the best outcomes when it comes to increasing collaboration between the Government and the private sector.

Question 3a. A number of witnesses at the hearing mentioned the shift to more disruptive and destructive cyber attacks. Over the last several years concern has been raised about the threat of nation-state cyber actors, criminals or others, causing physical damage through a cyber attack.

How difficult of an operation would this be, to cause physical damage, does it require a higher degree of sophistication?

Answer. Causing physical damage can, at times, require a higher degree of sophistication than simply obtaining access, but it depends on how well-defended a particular system may be. For example, an extremely well-defended system may be extremely difficult to access, but once accessed, it may be relatively easy to conduct actions upon; and the counter is also be true. The most important thing to note about this new trend towards cyber attacks that cause physical damage is that it is now happening. The capability to undertake such attacks is becoming more common and perhaps may end up in the hands of nation-states and other entities that are perhaps less subject to deterrence than typical, highly-capable cyber actors.

Question 3b. Can you speak to this threat and how concerned should we be about it?

Answer. This trend is one of the most troubling trends in cybersecurity because it represents a fundamental shift in the way cyber access to systems may be used, both as a tool for covert action, but also in a time of real conflict. Given the spread of these capabilities to less "deterrable" actors, we need to demonstrate that the United States takes such attacks seriously and will respond swiftly and with the application of all elements of National power, including military force, as needed in a particular circumstance.

Question 4a. As we look at evolving threats, ransomware attacks are on the rise. In your testimony, you noted that ransomware has been used by organized criminal groups and small actors alike.

Do you see the use of this tool growing?

Answer. As Microsoft recently noted, while the overall "volume of ransomware encounters is on a downward trend . . . a look at the attack vectors, the number of unique families released into the wild, and the improvements in malware code reveals otherwise."[1] As the Microsoft report points out, there was no decline in the volume of emails carrying ransomware downloaders; rather, systems operators were simply getting better at blocking the email entry point for such infections. Similarly, Microsoft notes that attackers continue to innovate and evolve the tools and tactics they use to deploy and exploit ransomware. As such, while numbers of successful attacks may be down, we have not seen the end of this trend.

Question 4b. Do you see ransomware being utilized by larger actors for more nefarious purposes?

Answer. Yes. There is possibility that we will see ransomware be put to larger-scale strategic use than the extraction of small amounts of wealth. It is important that governments and large corporations prepare for such incidents by establishing policies and procedures to prevent such attacks and the ability to recover if and when it happens.

Question 4c. How do we prepare and respond to ransomware attacks?

Answer. As with most cyber threats, the best offense is good preparation in advance and placing strong defensive measures in our networks. This includes basic hygiene at the outset: Consistent patching, use of strong passwords, two-factor authentication, strong anti-social engineering training of staff, as well as the deployment of strong capabilities using a defense-in-depth approach, from network and

---

[1] See Microsoft Malware Protection Center (MMPC) Ransomware: a Declining Nuisance or an Evolving Menace? (Feb. 14, 2017), available on-line at *https://blogs.technet.microsoft.com/mmpc/2017/02/14/ransomware-2016-threat-landscape-review/.*

end-point detection tools, to file security applications, use of strong encryption for sensitive data, and consistent, capable, and resilient back-up and recovery plans.

QUESTIONS FROM HONORABLE MIKE GALLAGHER FOR KEITH B. ALEXANDER

Question 1. General Alexander, at a cybersecurity panel in December 2016, in regards to problems with retention in the Federal cyber workforce, you were quoted as saying, "I do hear that people are increasingly leaving in large numbers and it is a combination of things that start with morale and there's now much more money on the outside . . . I am honestly surprised that some of these people in cyber companies make up to seven figures. That's five times what the chairman of the Joint Chiefs of Staff makes. Right? And these are people that are 32 years old . . . Do the math. [The NSA] has great competition." Several reasons have been cited for NSA and other cyber-related employees leaving the Government sector. These include: Higher pay in the private sector, low morale due to negative press coverage from leaked information regarding Government surveillance and data-collection capabilities, an overworked labor force which was described by an unnamed former U.S. cyber official as "20% of the workforce doing 80% of the actual work," to name just a few of the issues. What do you think are the biggest challenges facing the cybersecurity work force at present?

Answer. I think you identified a number of the challenges facing our Federal cybersecurity workforce, from higher pay on the outside, morale challenges as a result of recent disclosures and debates in the political arena, and a relatively severe lack of alignment in the number of positions and actual work being done. These negative factors are compounded when public officials "attack" the Government agencies and its personnel who are protecting the country for political gain.

We need to do a better job of encouraging cross-training between the public and private sectors by creating opportunities for people to move in and out of Government, maintaining their security clearances, and working to enhance both public and private-sector cybersecurity. Likewise, the Government needs to learn how to work better, more rapidly, and more flexibly with the most innovative companies in our Nation today, including those in various innovation hubs around the country.

This will not be easy, as the Government has real, legitimate concerns about protecting National security information, particularly as our companies become increasingly globalized. Until the Government harnesses the knowledge and capabilities of our Nation's most innovative thinkers, both by bringing them into the Government for short periods, as well as by working with the companies they start (and encouraging Government employees to do the same in the opposite direction), I fear that we will remain slow to innovate and adapt.

Finally, we need to recognize those protecting our Nation are doing what we asked them to do. We need to support them when the going gets tough. We should hold them accountable when they make mistakes, but we should clearly help them accomplish those missions we have asked them to accomplish.

Question 2. Russia's cyber attack in December 2015 against Ukraine's power grid is a concerning example of exposing weaknesses in physical systems that are connected to networks. What is in greater danger of offensive cyber operations by our adversaries: Our cyber networks themselves and the data stored in those networks, or physical systems that are connected to and dependent upon those networks to successfully operate?

Answer. Both the data stored in our computer systems and the physical systems they are connected to are subject to major threat from offensive cyber operations by our adversaries. American innovation economy, information and intellectual property is often as (or more) valuable than physical assets even though we do not often treat it as such. We cannot deny the troubling trend of physical damage being caused by cyber attacks. We need to act now to deter attacks that target core American National security interests, including, destructive cyber attacks, the massive theft of private-sector intellectual property, and efforts to obtain long-term access to critical infrastructure systems that might be exploited down the road.

Question 3a. In June 2015, I, along with millions of other Federal employees, became the victim of a cyber attack, as my personal data was hacked through the Office of Personnel Management. Putting this many Government employees' personal information at risk should have never happened.

What actions can we take to improve data encryption across all Federal networks?

Answer. Certainly, encrypting such data provides a certain amount of protection and there is no reason we ought not do so at scale. Encouraging broad adoption requires highly capable tools and a well-trained workforce with leadership willing to commit resources to the effort. We have challenges in these areas across the Government.

Encryption is only one type of protection that we should employ. When it comes to cybersecurity, Federal Government must become better and faster. There are pockets of excellence when it comes to both cyber offense and defense in the Federal Government and we should take advantage of that knowledge, capability, and skill set when it comes to protecting Federal systems.

In addition, the Government should leverage the best and brightest in the private sector and be able to work with them rapidly to innovate better defensive systems. The Government remains stuck in old paradigms of how security clearances are utilized and old contracting and requirements constructs when it comes to working with the private sector. If we are ever going to be able to innovate rapidly enough to keep up with the threats, we need to evolve to a much more modern mentality in the Government.

Question 3b. Are we simply lacking encryption in certain areas or is what we currently employ not good enough?

Answer. I do not think the issue is the lack of encryption strength, but rather a lack of capable tools and willingness and leadership to deploy such tools where they do exist. Moreover, though, I am concerned that the lack of a strong working relationship day in and day out between our most innovative Government agencies and our most innovative private-sector entities is hampering the success of our overall defensive effort as a Nation. We can and must do more here and I stand ready to work with this committee to achieve this critical goal for our Nation.

Also, we should consider outsourcing the IT infrastructure and consolidating cybersecurity for the civilian side of Government.

Question 4. My colleague, Congressman Hurd, has proposed the creation of a Cyber Defense National Guard. In August 2016, Congressman Hurd suggested, "The Federal Government could forgive the student loan debt of STEM graduates who agreed to work for a specified number of years in the Federal Government in cybersecurity jobs at places like SSA or Department of the Interior. Furthermore, when those individuals moved on to private-sector jobs they would commit 1 weekend a month and 2 weeks a year to continued Federal service. This would help ensure a cross-pollination of experience between the private and public sectors." What do you think of Congressman Hurd's proposal?

Answer. I think that the type of cross-pollination that Congressman Hurd proposes is a sensible approach to consider, as the incentive in this proposal would also provide more students to train in critical STEM areas that would also be helpful to our National security (including our economic security) in the long run. This would also ensure a steady stream of exceptional personnel into the Government, even if it is for a few years.

While there are important questions we must examine when it comes to our fiscal situation, from a cybersecurity and National security perspective, I am supportive of new and innovative ideas like those proposed by Congressman Hurd and wish to continue to work with you, Congressman Hurd, Chairman McCaul, Ranking Member Thompson, and others on this committee and across Congress to support and move forward such good ideas.

QUESTIONS FROM CHAIRMAN MICHAEL T. MCCAUL FOR MICHAEL DANIEL

Question 1a. While the goal, for combatting cyber crime, is to make it financially untenable to conduct illegal activities, what would the corollary of this goal be for nation state actors?

Answer. Deterrence for all cyber criminals, including nation-state actors, must start with increasing the cost to conduct an attack and associated likelihood of success. This can only be accomplished by disrupting the adversaries' business models. Although re-engineering malware requires some time and effort, it is relatively easy to make small tweaks so that it can evade detection. However, an adversaries' total suite of indicators (including tactics, techniques, and procedures, and typical operational approach) is much more difficult to change and update. By exposing adversaries' predictable malicious activity and enabling infrastructure, we can force adversaries, both nation-state and other actors, to adapt their business model. Business reengineering is a much more time-consuming and resource-intensive task that more effective disrupts malicious activity better than any technological solution.

Question 1b. How do we tip the scales so that it isn't worth it for nation-state actors to break into our systems both in the private sector and in the Government?

Answer. As stated above, deterring nation-state actors starts with increasing their overall costs by upending their business model. We need to start by removing known, low-level actors from the ecosystem by disrupting known, preventable attacks. Removing low-level actors also makes it harder for less sophisticated nation-states to enter into the criminal arena. By lowering the noise, we can focus on the more sophisticated nation-states and actors. The Cyber Threat Alliance has a critical role to play in this disruption through their creation of Playbooks that give visibility into adversaries' infrastructure, TTPs, and business processes. By sharing information, CTA members can better protect customers across the globe in all economic sectors.

However, I strongly believe that governments build on these private sector-led technical disruption efforts with diplomacy, economic tools (such as sanctions), law enforcement actions, intelligence activity, and if necessary, military action in order for technical actions to be effective.

Question 2a. At the hearing, we heard that we need to rethink how the Government and private sector relate to one another on cyber issues.

What are your recommendations for rethinking the relationship between public and private sectors?

Answer. Public-private partnerships are necessary to tackle the cyber challenge. While governments have unique tools to combat cyber crime in the form of diplomacy and law enforcement, the development and deployment of technological tools primarily fall to the private sector. Therefore, the focus must be on public-private collaboration and partnership, not just regulation or contracting. Effective collaboration requires us to be more realistic about what governments can and should be doing. Governments have a unique responsibility and authority to take action beyond the technological defense of networks. Defining roles and responsibilities for both private and public stakeholders empowers both groups to be most effective in combatting cyber adversaries.

Question 2b. How do we ensure the private and public sectors can work together harmoniously, without overstepping the Government's role or creating a new regulatory regime?

Answer. As discussed above, the Government can bring to bear authorities and capabilities in diplomacy, law enforcement, and intelligence, as well as technical defensive capabilities. These capabilities should be used in conjunction with the capabilities for rapid defensive action that the private sector can bring to bear. Given its position in society, the Government must also play a role in convening and promoting best practices that reduce cyber risk. An example of such an initiative is the NIST-led process to build the Cyber Security Framework. This example shows how the Government can work with industry to identify best practices that are not mandatory. Best practices developed in public-private collaboration will have cross-sector applicability to achieve risk reduction across all critical infrastructure sectors. Cybersecurity-related regulations also have a place in certain industries, but such approaches should be used sparingly and with maximum flexibility. Such regulations should be risk-based and not compliance-focused. Compliance-based regulation has the potential to divert an organization's resources from driving down risk.

Question 2c. How can we ensure this much-needed and strengthened collaboration is nimble enough to consider the evolving nature of cyber threats and organizational needs?

Answer. Taking a risk-based approach is the solution to ensuring that the public and private collaboration remain nimble and effective. The NIST Framework development process and end result should serve as a model for future efforts. The risk-based approach in the NIST Framework ensures that all organizations, regardless of industry, size, maturity, can adequately baseline, benchmark, and strengthen their cyber posture. The flexibility of this approach empowers organizations to align resources to drive down risk, versus spending resources to demonstrate compliance.

Question 3a. How is the Federal Government engaging its international partners and allies regarding cyber norms?

What should the Government do to more clearly define cyber norms?

Answer. The NIST development approach is not only a proven model for domestic public-private collaboration, but also for broader international engagement. In addition to this collaborative model, muti-lateral efforts also have demonstrated success. This includes the G7 increasingly promoting common values around internet freedom and cybersecurity. Furthermore, bi-lateral agreements, such as President Obama and President Xi defining appropriate and inappropriate use of assets in the cyber space, are effective for working closely with key individual nation.

Question 3b. How can the private sector engage in this work?

Answer. The private sector absolutely has a role in these efforts to define cyber norms. The perspective of cybersecurity operators is essential to ensuring that international cyber norms are appropriately actionable, scalable, and applicable across the globe. To date, we've seen private-sector input incorporated in a range of Track 1.5 and Track 2 dialogues. These various efforts must be continued to ensure harmonious collaboration between the public and private sectors.

Question 4a. You stated in your testimony that hacktivists, criminals, and nation-states are moving to more destructive and disruptive activities.

Why do you think this is happening?

Answer. In the simplest terms, because they can. Motivations differ among groups, however. For criminal actors, money forms the prime motivation, while hacktivists want to make a point publicly, and nation-states want to either conduct espionage or hold other nations at risk to achieve their foreign policy or national security goals. Each of these groups are learning that more disruptive and destructive activities have a higher likelihood of achieving their goal, and little downside exists for moving to the more destructive techniques. In addition, destruction and disruption is increasingly happening in mass due to adversaries having increased access to open-source or low-cost tools at their disposal. Finally, neither the public or private sector is adequately deterring adversaries at a technical level. As discussed in an above question, there must be a concerted effort to lower the noise in the system by taking out low-level actors.

Question 4b. Where does this trend move in the future and do we continue to see even more destructive and disruptive attacks?

Answer. Continued interconnectivity will continue to increase cyber threats. We live in a digital age that promises incredible efficiencies and productivity, but it also brings new challenges and potential vulnerabilities that—left unchecked—threaten to undermine these very benefits. As connectivity continues to increase, the cyber threat will become broader, more frequent, and more dangerous. The growth in volume of connective devices will make effective cyber defense even harder from a sheer numbers perspective. This fact, paired with the fact that the barriers to entry are low and the potential return on investment is fairly high, means that malicious cyber activity is increasing dramatically and will continue to grow for the foreseeable future.

Question 4c. How do we prepare for and defend against this trend?

Answer. Response was not received at the time of publication.

QUESTIONS FROM HONORABLE MIKE GALLAGHER FOR MICHAEL DANIEL

Question 1. Russia's cyber attack in December 2015 against Ukraine's power grid is a concerning example of exposing weaknesses in physical systems that are connected to networks. What is in greater danger of offensive cyber operations by our adversaries: Our cyber networks themselves and the data stored in those networks, or physical systems that are connected to and dependent upon those networks to successfully operate?

Answer. A blanket statement cannot be made about whether network or physical system assets are most vulnerable. Instead, we must conduct risk assessments across all critical infrastructure assets by evaluating potential cyber threats, vulnerabilities, and consequences. This process will enable the Government and private sector to prioritize resources in order to most efficiently and effectively reduce risk. The risk assessment must consider and prioritize the need to build trust where money is serviced and where critical services are deployed.

Question 2a. In June 2015, I, along with millions of other Federal employees, became the victim of a cyber attack, as my personal data was hacked through the Office of Personnel Management. Putting this many Government employees' personal information at risk should have never happened.

What actions can we take to improve data encryption across all Federal networks?

Answer. Improving the security of antiquated networks must be a priority for the Government. However, encryption alone is not an adequate solution to enhance network security. In fact, stronger encryption would not have necessarily prevented the OPM breach, as the hackers were able to obtain administrative privileges. Because they had those credentials, they could operate as trusted insiders and by-pass or turn off the encryption. Once intruders have access to legitimate credentials, encryption is not usually a barrier.

Question 2b. Are we simply lacking encryption in certain areas or is what we currently employ not good enough?

Answer. Strengthening encryption is only aspect of improved security. Organizations need to employ a risk-based, holistic approach to managing their cybersecurity that involves multiple methods for frustrating the malicious actors. For example, organizations should manage privileged access carefully, enable appropriate network segmentation, and employ sophisticated detection capabilities to protect their highest-value assets.

Question 3. My colleague, Congressman Hurd, has proposed the creation of a Cyber Defense National Guard. In August 2016, Congressman Hurd suggested, "The Federal Government could forgive the student loan debt of STEM graduates who agreed to work for a specified number of years in the Federal Government in cybersecurity jobs at places like SSA or Department of the Interior. Furthermore, when those individuals moved on to private-sector jobs they would commit 1 weekend a month and 2 weeks a year to continued Federal service. This would help ensure a cross-pollination of experience between the private and public sectors." What do you think of Congressman Hurd's proposal?

Answer. There is certainly a need to encourage people to pursue fields related to cybersecurity. Without reviewing the Congressman's proposal in detail, this program sounds like an innovative idea to strengthen and grow the cyber workforce. However, efforts to close the cyber talent gap must be broader than just focused on attracting talent to the Government. In additional to considering this specific proposal, we should also review existing initiatives to determine how we can best expand on programs already in place. Furthermore, neither the Government nor private sector can "hire out" of this problem. Instead, we must focus on evolving the workforce and enabling greater automation. Energy should be focused on developing workforce strategies that harness human intelligence, sophistication, and action.

QUESTIONS FROM CHAIRMAN MICHAEL T. MCCAUL FOR FRANK J. CILLUFFO

Question 1. While the goal, for combatting cyber crime, is to make it financially untenable to conduct illegal activities, what would the corollary of this goal be for nation-state actors?

How do we tip the scales so that it isn't worth it for nation-state actors to break into our systems both in the private sector and in the Government?

Answer. Response was not received at the time of publication.

Question 2a. At the hearing, we heard that we need to rethink how the Government and private sector relate to one another on cyber issues.

What are your recommendations for rethinking the relationship between public and private sectors?

Question 2b. How do we ensure the private and public sectors can work together harmoniously, without overstepping the Government's role or creating a new regulatory regime?

Question 2c. How can we ensure this much-needed and strengthened collaboration is nimble enough to consider the evolving nature of cyber threats and organizational needs?

Answer. Response was not received at the time of publication.

Question 3a. In your testimony you noted that "In Russia, the forces of crime, business, and politics have long converged in a toxic blend; and there is evidence of complicity between the Russian government and cyber criminals and hackers." The recent DOJ indictment of two Russian FSB officers also alluded to this government/security service collaboration with cyber criminals. This blurring of the lines makes attribution a much taller task.

Can you expand on why this is such a dangerous problem?

Question 3b. Are we seeing this in other countries?

Question 3c. What can the United States do to combat this?

Answer. Response was not received at the time of publication.

Question 4. When discussing criminal enterprises you noted that the gap between the capabilities of sophisticated cyber criminals and nation-states is increasingly narrowing. You also noted the cross-border interjurisdictional approach needed to take down Avalanche criminal network. It seems like in light of the growth in the criminal enterprise we should expect more threats in this area. How do we ensure and support international collaboration to address these criminal entities?

Answer. Response was not received at the time of publication.

QUESTIONS FROM HONORABLE MIKE GALLAGHER FOR FRANK J. CILLUFFO

Question 1. Russia's cyber attack in December 2015 against Ukraine's power grid is a concerning example of exposing weaknesses in physical systems that are connected to networks. What is in greater danger of offensive cyber operations by our adversaries: Our cyber networks themselves and the data stored in those networks, or physical systems that are connected to and dependent upon those networks to successfully operate?

Answer. Response was not received at the time of publication.

Question 2a. In June 2015, I, along with millions of other Federal employees, became the victim of a cyber attack, as my personal data was hacked through the Office of Personnel Management. Putting this many Government employees' personal information at risk should have never happened.

What actions can we take to improve data encryption across all Federal networks?

Question 2b. Are we simply lacking encryption in certain areas or is what we currently employ not good enough?

Answer. Response was not received at the time of publication.

Question 3. My colleague, Congressman Hurd, has proposed the creation of a Cyber Defense National Guard. In August 2016, Congressman Hurd suggested, "The Federal Government could forgive the student loan debt of STEM graduates who agreed to work for a specified number of years in the Federal Government in cyber-security jobs at places like SSA or Department of the Interior. Furthermore, when those individuals moved on to private-sector jobs they would commit 1 weekend a month and 2 weeks a year to continued Federal service. This would help ensure a cross-pollination of experience between the private and public sectors." What do you think of Congressman Hurd's proposal?

Answer. Response was not received at the time of publication.

QUESTIONS FROM CHAIRMAN MICHAEL T. MCCAUL FOR BRUCE W. MCCONNELL

Question 1. While the goal, for combatting cyber crime, is to make it financially untenable to conduct illegal activities, what would the corollary of this goal be for nation-state actors?

How do we tip the scales so that it isn't worth it for the nation-state actors to break into our systems both in the private sector and in the Government?

Answer. The conventional wisdom as articulated by the Department of State and the White House is that we should employ all instruments of National power to deter cyber attacks from nation-states. These instruments include the traditional "DIME" four-some—diplomatic, intelligence, military, and economic— to which law enforcement is usually added in the cyber context. We have seen that approach used with some success to lead up to the agreement between Presidents Xi and Obama regarding economic espionage conducted by cyber means.

However, we also know that deterrence in cyber space is quite challenging, particularly for an advanced, connected economy like the United States. We have much more to lose in a degraded cyber environment than almost anyone else. Further, as the witnesses testified, while cyber defense is important, today, and for the foreseeable future, "Offense Wins." For these reasons I advocated that the United States begin to propose measures of restraint in the development and use of cyber weapons. There is an emerging international consensus that, for example, attacks on international infrastructure such as core internet routers or key financial exchanges and clearing houses, is detrimental to all nations and should be off-limits. The United States, by virtue of its position as the world's strongest cyber power, is in the best position to lead by example and drive public advocacy for the adoption of such cyber norms of behavior.

Question 2a. At the hearing, we heard that we need to rethink how the Government and private sector relate to one another on cyber issues.

What are your recommendations for rethinking the relationship between public and private sectors?

Question 2b. How do we ensure the private and public sectors can work together harmoniously, without overstepping the Government's role or creating a new regulatory regime?

Question 2c. How can we ensure this much-needed and strengthened collaboration is nimble enough to consider the evolving nature of cyber threats and organizational needs?

Answer. Strengthening agile public-private collaboration is a continuing challenge. Recently-enacted laws, sponsored by this committee, have created improved incentives for such collaboration. But there is no silver bullet. The potential for conflicts of interest, litigation and liability risk, and unintended consequences remains large. Perhaps the best way forward is to increase the exchange of people between Government and the private sector. With shared experience, many seemingly intractable differences can be addressed with creative, informal solutions that respect the policy and economic environments of both sides.

As far as a new regulatory regime, in my view some additional regulation will be needed, as illustrated recently by the State of New York for financial services companies. This approach—having regulation proposed and adopted by the expert regulatory agency, is preferable to any across-the-board approach. Given the variable risks and business models of different critical infrastructure sectors, one size will not fit all.

Question 3. In your testimony you posed an interesting set of questions related to the Internet of Things (IoT) or the Internet of Everything (IoE), specifically: "Why do we assume the bad guys will own the sensor network? Why not have the good guys own it and use the knowledge of what is happening on the internet to increase security?" So, I have to ask you and our other witnesses, what are the key elements of ensuring the good guys own the network and the data and information derived?

Answer. Thank you. I believe there are three elements that would increase the likelihood that the good guys own the network. First, the endpoints need to be smarter and more secure, including the ability to be modified or turned off remotely with appropriate authorization. The technical standards community is working on this, but it could use a push from Government. Second, the network service providers, such as the Tier 1 Carriers, need the authority to see the network status information that the devices provide and the authority to stop bad traffic (as they do now with spam). There would need to be liability protection and business model changes for this to be practical. Finally, there need to be strong and enforceable privacy provisions in statute so that any bad actors who may work for the good guy organizations don't abuse the capabilities that the first two items require.

QUESTIONS FROM HONORABLE MIKE GALLAGHER FOR BRUCE W. MCCONNELL

Question 1. Russia's cyber attack in December 2015 against Ukraine's power grid is a concerning example of exposing weaknesses in physical systems that are connected to networks. What is in greater danger of offensive cyber operations by our adversaries: Our networks themselves and the data stored in those networks, or physical systems that are connected to and dependent upon those networks to successfully operate?

Answer. If one equates "danger" and "risk," then one can consider the three elements of risk: Threat, vulnerability, and consequence. Threat, in turn, is comprised of capability and intent. So the question is, which exhibits the larger combination of these risk elements: The networks themselves or the physical systems connected to them?

The table below reflects my current thinking.

Risk Element	Networks	Physical Systems
Threat: Intent	Malicious actors may be less interested in attacking the core networks because they depend on them also.	Malicious actors may find the possible visible consequences of successful physical attacks more attractive than the less visible results of network attacks.
Threat: Capability	Widespread availability of attack tools means that a well-funded and persistent actor can inflict significant damage, at least for brief periods.	Knowledge of how to attack physical systems is not wide-spread. The systems are diverse and often peculiar.
Vulnerability	Most critical networks are highly defended, continually updated and patched, and monitored with a 24x7 dedicated security culture.	Physical systems rely on older software and hardware, and the long replacement cycles mean these systems are softer targets, at least once an attacker has learned how the systems work.
Consequences	Since both the networks themselves and the physical systems depend on the networks, the consequences of major network failures could be catastrophic.	Physical systems tend to be loosely interconnected and in some ways locally managed. Thus a system-wide failure is less likely, at least in some sectors. Regional effects are more likely. However, service restoration time could be longer as some scarce components may not be easily replaceable.

Question 2a. In June 2015, I, along with millions of other Federal employees became the victim of a cyber attack, as my personal data was hacked through the Office of Personnel Management. Putting this many Government employees' personal information at risk should have never happened.

What actions can we take to improve data encryption across all Federal networks?

Question 2b. Are we simply lacking encryption in certain areas or is what we currently employ not good enough?

Answer. Strong encryption and strong (multi-factor) authentication should be mandatory for systems as critical as the one you refer to. One must select strong encryption and implement it uniformly and well. The current Federal encryption standards provide strong enough encryption for Unclassified systems. However, agency implementation is likely to be non-uniform and, in some cases, technically incorrect. It is by no means obvious that line agencies whose missions are not cyber-security could successfully implement such a policy, were it in place. Recent proposals to centralize some aspects of cybersecurity responsibility in a civilian agency have merit in this context.

Question 3. My colleague, Congressman Hurd, has proposed the creation of a Cyber Defense National Guard. In August 2016, Congressman Hurd suggested, "The Federal Government could forgive the student loan debt of STEM graduates who agreed to work for a specified number of years in the Federal Government in cyber-security jobs at places like SSA or Department of the Interior. Furthermore, when those individuals moved on to private-sector jobs they would commit 1 weekend a month or 2 weeks a year to continued Federal service. This would help ensure a cross-pollination of experience between the private and public sectors." What do you think of Congressman Hurd's proposal?

Answer. While serving at the Department of Homeland Security, I was engaged in lengthy discussions along with the Department of Defense about the possibilities of a cyber National Guard, a cyber reserves, and a cyber volunteer corps of some sort. Each of these ideas has advantages and disadvantages based on existing law and policy regarding the use of civilian citizens to perform security duties, potential for conflicts of interest, costs, etc. Perhaps this is an area that the Congressional Research Service could be helpful in investigating.

○

www.ingramcontent.com/pod-product-compliance
Lightning Source LLC
Chambersburg PA
CBHW080857260726
48660CB00009B/3346